C000140843

I Did It
In My Pyjamas

ANGELA DE SOUZA

BISAC: BUS025000
Business & Economics / Entrepreneurship
ISBN-13: 978-1505662689
ISBN-10: 1505662680

"No one can make you feel inferior without your permission."

- Eleanor Roosevelt

Contents

Introduction

"Most people are about as happy as they make up their minds to be."

\- Abraham Lincoln

There are no recipes.

Very often, I get asked about the rules and how to's of business, such as: How do I build my business? How can I get more sales? How can I make more money quickly? How did you do it? It seems everyone wants the recipe or the map for a shortcut to instant wealth and success. Several people claim that they have the recipe and map, which, for a hefty sum, they will share with you. I honestly believe that there aren't any recipes or maps and I would go as far as to say that there are also very few rules. This is how I built my business, the Women's Business Club, and what you are about to read is my ongoing journey with all its ups downs, successes and failures.

When it comes to business, few people ask the right questions. Think about it – if we all followed a set of rules, there would be no creativity, no innovation, and no fun! Some rules were made to be broken. Odds are meant to be defied. Methods should be challenged. However, some rules *must* be obeyed or we will end up in chaos. A great business leader will know which rules to break and which rules to respect. I honour the laws of our land, especially parking rules and the speed limit. Apart from the fact that it is dangerous to ignore them, I particularly don't like paying fines! These are rules that I am not willing to break because I don't want to bear the consequences of breaking them. Other rules that I particularly like to adhere to is the zero of my bank balance. Messing with the zero and the unarranged overdraft costs bank charges, affects my credit rating, and can lead to a great deal of inconvenience if payments can't be made. So I don't mess around with that one either – I stay as far away from zero as possible.

However, I break the rules of dress code regularly. Many mornings I simply don't get dressed and work at home in my pyjamas. In winter, I can even be found in bed with my laptop and mobile phone, conducting business as usual. Those who know me also know that I can be found working in the bathtub or on a hilltop. Who says you have to work in an office between nine and five? My best work is done at 5am or 11pm on some days. These are rules that I have no problem breaking and I refuse to conform to the conventional nine to five.

And don't get me started on the traditional business plan! I break most of the rules there and teach others to do so too when their personality type requires me to do so. However, I also teach other personality type business owners how to write a traditional business plan. In a nutshell, I try to do what is best for a particular individual or business and not what everyone else is doing. Lorah-Kelly, my daughter, photographer and owner of the Cheltenham Women's Business Club, struggled to be inspired by her business plan. Without giving it a thought, I told her to buy a scrapbook and do it scrapbook style. The results were phenomenal; she actually loved every minute of creating her business plan and injected fresh creativity into her business. Why? Because we broke the rules and threw the "recipe" out of the window!

I Did It In My Pyjamas is my story of how I built the Women's Business Club from nothing to the national success it is today. I have by no means arrived but write this almost as a travel diary of my journey to share what I have learned and am still learning. This is not a recipe book and does not contain a magic formula for how to get rich quickly. "Seven steps" do not exist, and any numbered list within these pages is simply to make reading a little easier, not to prescribe the exact way to run a business. You are very welcome to add your own points to my lists or disregard points you disagree with. This is my story and I hope it inspires you to write your story in your own way. I did it in my pyjamas. How are you building your business?

Enjoy!

I Did it With Zero Capital

"The life of money-making is one undertaken under compulsion since wealth is not the good we are seeking and is merely useful for the sake of something else."

- Aristotle

It doesn't take money to make money.

o what if you have money or don't have money? That has little to do with it. What matters is *what* you want and, even more importantly, *why* you want it. From there, the money will come, if and when you need it.

How to Start With Nothing

Before we get started with how to start with nothing, let me ask you a very important question. If you were given a lump sum of money, what would you do with it? On many occasions, I have had an opportunity to enter a competition or win an award that comes with a cash pay-out. Each time, I have asked myself what I would do with the money if I won, and each time I discovered that I didn't actually *need* more money. Note – there's a difference between *wanting* and *needing*! At times I needed to fine tune my strategy; at other times I needed to appoint people to carry some of the load; and at other times I simply needed a break to get a fresh perspective. If on any of those occasions I had been presented with more money, I may have wasted it as I wasn't ready for it. From the time I started my business up until now, I have always had the right amount of money at any given time. If I were given money right this minute, or earned an unexpected fee, I would simply pop it into a savings account or invest it so it would be available when I needed it. More money isn't going to grow my business this year. My plan is to consistently keep on doing what I did last year with a few exciting new projects thrown in the mix to keep it fun. None of what I have planned requires more money but when I am ready to launch my fantastic new product range and need money for capital, I will simply dip into what I have purposefully saved up for this next stage.

So, my question to you again is, what do you need money for right now? Will it solve a real problem or will it hinder the creative process that will force you to innovate? Food for thought, isn't it? Innovation often comes from difficult times when a problem presents itself and you don't have the money to solve it. Too often, money is actually your worst enemy, as you don't have to innovate to get out of a hole; you simply throw money at the problem to make it go away.

"It's all well and good telling me all the fluffy stuff," I hear you saying, "but how do I practically make money, starting with absolutely nothing at all?"

Well, I am so pleased you asked! For me, it's very simple; my *guiding light* is to always keep my expenses less than my income. So, to start a business with nothing means that you have to start with income and not an expense. Even though I don't know your financial situation, I am quite certain that you already have enough money right now to start a business – even if enough means absolutely nothing. You already have exactly what you need. The question is, can you see it, and are you creative enough to do something with it? If in doubt, skip ahead to the chapter called "I Did It in the Bath" and then come back to this point. You see, if you are truly an entrepreneur then nothing will stop you from building a business. No excuses will hold you back. No fears will be strong enough to keep you where you are. You are who you are and what is inside of you will naturally come out *if* you allow it to.

An artist will create art; a writer will write; a musician will make music, even without training, although their art, writing and music will be naturally better if they invest in their gift. A leader will lead, a manager will manage, an engineer will pull things apart, just to see how they are made, and an entrepreneur WILL set up a business. Who you are and the gift inside of you will emerge naturally *if* you allow it to, and it will thrive if you train and nurture it. The problem is that most people are trying so hard to be who they think they *should* be that they don't see who they really are. Who are you?

What is inside of you? What comes naturally? What do you love to do? What are you most passionate about? These are the most important questions, not the question of how much capital you have to start with. Let's take a look at how Richard Branson started his Virgin empire.

Take Payment First.

In 1969, Richard was living in a London commune, which was infested with the British music and drug scene. It was there that he had the idea to begin a mail-order record company to help fund his magazine. Richard then went on to start what became known as Virgin Records. He achieved this with little start-up money because he *first* took the payment for the records and then went out to buy them – this solved his cash flow problem and enabled him to build it into the brand that he sold for around £560 million. He sold Virgin Records to help fund his next venture, Virgin Airlines.

Many great entrepreneurs did not have a large amount of capital available to them at first. And yet they persevered anyway. What can we learn from these people? What did they have that led them to ultimate success, if not money?

So What *Does* It Take To Make Money?

If all it took was money to make more money then why don't lottery winners all have a significant amount of wealth piled up? Money *can* make more money but only in the hands of the right person. However, the right person can make money with or without having money in the first place. So clearly, the key lies in being the right person, as opposed to having an initial investment.

"The key lies in being the right person, as opposed to having an initial investment."

I have had money and lost money over and over again, but it took years to learn to become a person that can handle money and make it grow. Being the right person is a lifelong journey once you find the path. Too many business owners are so busy trying to make money that they haven't even considered whether they are on the wrong path in the first place. It's easy to say that it doesn't take money to make money and it also leaves the burning question "Then, what *does* it take to make money?"

Let me share what I believe it takes to make money with you and, at the same time, back it up with observations and stories from people that have made and sustained wealth.

1. Authenticity

As Judy Garland so rightly said, "*Always be a first-rate version of yourself and not a second-rate version of someone else.*"

Authenticity is important, particularly in business. You need to have a personality of your own, one that draws people toward you. Over the years in business I have met some people who came across as authentic and others who seem to have lost themselves. Some years ago I met a man (let's call him Tom) at a networking event and when the time came for us to introduce ourselves to each other all he talked about was making money. Now I know business is about making money but that's not all it's about! This man had clearly lost the ability to talk about anything that made him *real* and interesting. In fact, Tom's constant referral to his love of money was blatantly off-putting. Over the months that passed after this encounter, I found that many people did not speak very highly of him and some were even very bruised from how much he had hurt them in business. We will return to Tom and the subject of money later in the book.

On the flip side, I met an amazing woman – let's call her Lucy – who seemed to be the real deal and was indeed very successful. In my brief encounter with her, I felt drawn to her. She never once mentioned money but she spoke of her passion in a way that made her eyes light up. As she gave me a tour of her factory, I noticed how kindly she treated every single staff member and how much they seemed to like and respect her. She wore a simple dress and her hair was bunched up loosely on her head. Not that any of this matters, of course, but it did give me the clear notion that she had nothing to prove and wasn't trying to impress me or anyone else. Where Tom had repelled me, Lucy made me feel drawn to her. I have met many men and women like Tom and Lucy. Some men have impressed me and some have repulsed me, some women have impressed me and some have made me run in the opposite direction as quickly and as far as possible. All have made money, which showed that they are indeed businessmen and women. One of the main differences between the two groups of people that I have personally observed is simply authenticity. The people that draw me to them are not trying to make money as their primary objective; they are doing what they love and the money has simply been a by-product.

The most powerful thing that you have to offer the world is the authentic you. You are indisputably original. Understanding your value will unlock your potential and take you to places that you never dreamed possible.

"The most powerful thing that you have to offer the world is the authentic you. You are indisputably original. Understanding your value will unlock your potential and take you to places that you never dreamed possible."

Unlocking *you* will be the most amazing and liberating experience you will ever have! There is nothing quite like being completely satisfied with who you are and what you do with every day of your life. Consider this fantastic concept, written by Liggy Webb, author of *Resilience*:

A bar of iron costs £5
Made into horseshoes, it can be worth about £20
Made into needles, it can increase its value to £3,500
Made into balance springs for watches, its value can leap to £250,000.

We are far more valuable than a bar of iron, aren't we? But how much value do we allow ourselves to have? Are we reaching our full potential or are we settling for the minimum? Let me share a little nugget of truth with you. You ARE valuable. You might still be at the "bar of iron" stage, or perhaps you have been moulded into a metaphorical horseshoe already, but ultimately, you and I have the potential to become the most valuable item on the list if we allow our authenticity to shine through. Staying authentic means we stay true to ourselves, to our purpose, and to our underlying passion. This takes me onto my next point... passion.

2. **Passion**

With passion, you can sell ice to an Eskimo or sand in the desert! Passion sells. True passion is authentic and people like what is real. Passionate people glow when they speak about their passion; their eyes light up and they seem to have an energy about them when they speak. It is always great to be in the company of someone who is truly passionate about what they do in life. Are you passionate about what you do? Can people instantly tell what excites you in life? If you are not sure, why not ask a few people to share their observations with you about what they perceive to be your passion in life?

It is passion that will help you persevere through the tough times in business that will come your way. You cannot avoid the tough times; business and life in general are a constant rollercoaster ride. Passion gets you through the lows, helps you stand firm when it seems everyone is against you, and holds you to your course when confusion tries to knock you off your rails.

"Don't ask yourself what the world needs; ask yourself what makes you come alive. And then go and do that. Because what the world needs is people who have come alive."

- Howard Thurman

Passion Killers

It's all well and good having passion in abundance but what happens when you meet face to face with issues that will try to deflate your passion, like a needle pricking a balloon? Here are some "passion killers", as I like to call them, that you need to be ready to deal with.

Burnout

All work and no play kills passion. Burnout can seem like you just don't have the energy to carry on. You run out of steam. You run out of inspiration and creativity. The passion that you had when you started your business has faded and you feel like you are stuck with no way forward. Burnout is very common in small businesses where the business owner has to do everything, from making the tea to finalising the year's accounts and, somewhere in between, find time to actually do the work that brings the money in too. Passion easily dies when the business owner is burnt out.

Avoid burnout by immediately stopping to have a break if you realise that you are heading towards burnout. If you are already burned out and are just going through the motions each day, then stop. Stop, stop, stop! Go out, have some fun, get a hobby, spend time with friends and family, try something new and laugh as much as possible. Burnout can be a form of depression and there are many more tips in the chapter, *I Did It With Depression*.

The bottom line is that lack of passion will only harm your business and push you even further down into a black hole, so take action and do something about it urgently. Talk to someone about how you feel, see a doctor, engage in self-help or read inspirational books.

Criticism

Feedback and criticism can be extremely useful as well as extremely hurtful. When we hear something negative, we instantly feel like a failure and don't remember the many compliments that we so often get. Instead, we focus entirely on the one person who was not happy with us, our product or service. Sleepless nights follow as we toss and turn over one person's opinion – attention we sadly never give to positive feedback. Internalising criticism can kill passion. It is essential that we take it on the chin, improve where necessary, apologise when called for, and move on. Criticism is a part of the business journey; it will always come your way, no matter how wonderful you are and no matter how great your business is. How criticism affects you is entirely your choice.

"Criticism is a part of the business journey; it will always come your way, no matter how wonderful you are and no matter how great your business is. How criticism affects you is entirely your choice."

I used to struggle with criticism and it could take many days for me to get over a comment, or even a perceived disappointment from a client. Being wrong killed me inside, piece by piece, as I hated letting people down. The great thing is that as soon as I realised it was a problem, that it was unhealthy, I began to work on it. Things didn't instantly get better – it was a part of my journey and took time – but today, I take criticism much better and do my best to always use it to my advantage. My concern is not what people think of me but who I am becoming, and if criticism can help me become an even better version of me then I will use it. It is always my choice and I will always do my best to use my choice to take everything that comes my way to mould me into a better person.

Complacency
Lack of change, direction, focus or goals can kill passion. When you get nowhere in what you are doing, you will lose passion. Keep reinventing your business, stay ahead of the curve, and be creative with your business. Most importantly, have a lot of fun! Complacency often occurs when a

business is on top, the market leader, or peaking. At this stage, it is easy to become complacent, but it is just as easy to fall right down to the bottom of the market if you are not careful. Laziness is very close to complacency too; you have "made it" in your eyes and so you get lazy and lose your edge. Stay ahead of your competitors and resist complacency, keep your passion alive and keep working on something new and exciting. Your competitors are always watching you, learning from you, and trying to get ahead of you. If you become complacent, they may overtake you. Don't assume you will always be the best, don't assume you will always be stable, and simply don't assume anything at all.

Fear

Wrongly placed fear does nothing but damage. The most common fear in business is the fear of failure, but other fears can include underlying fears that you are a fraud, that no one will pay for your products or services, that your competitors are better than you, and that you don't have what it takes to build a successful business. Business owners with wrongly placed fear tend to play it safe, resulting in their business barely keeping its head above water because their fears hold them back from achieving their full potential. The best business owners are comfortable with fear and use it to propel themselves forward. Fear is such a huge subject that I have dedicated an entire chapter to it, *I Did It With Fear*. Needless to say, fear kills passion!

Negative People

I had to sigh as I began this section. The pain and memories of negative people is still raw. Negative people are usually jealous of what you have achieved and who you have become. It has been a tough journey but I have learned not to listen to everything that negative people say. There is a fine line between constructive criticism and negativity, and it takes a great deal of practice to learn what to take to heart and what to ignore. Flattery is not negative but is just as damaging. In both cases – negativity and flattery – the person is not interested in your best interests, but in their best interests. They want to gain from you or put you down so that they can feel better about themselves. In both cases, take no notice. It would be rude to "show them the hand" but really you should do that, metaphorically. Take no notice, if possible. If it's not possible and a response is required, try the following:

Empathise with them

Show them that you care, even though you disagree. Be sincere with your empathy, as they often don't know that what they are doing is immature.

Avoid arguments

When they provoke you, keep your cool and refuse to argue. Find a way to diffuse the situation, no matter what it takes. Responding to an argument will only lower you to their level.

Offer kind words

A kind word truly does turn away wrath and you can counter their hostility with kindness. It may not show an immediate positive in your favour but, either long or short term, it will always trump negativity.

"Surround yourself with the best people you can find, delegate authority, and don't interfere, as long as the policy you've decided upon is being carried out."

- Ronald Reagan

Surround yourself with positive people and keep your passion alive. Positive people may say negative things but usually they are the truth and to your advantage. Find people you can trust so that, when you need to be confronted, you can take it. Positive people want to lift you up and not bring you down. Negative people want to bring you down and "put you in your place". Take time to learn the difference between the two so that you can take on board well-meaning feedback from positive people and disregard manipulative feedback from negative people.

3. Talent

Every single person is born with gifts and talents. Some have more than others do, but we all have them. Some use more than others, and that is what counts the most. Johann Wolfgang von Goethe said, "*The person born with a talent they are meant to use will find their greatest happiness in using it.*" Too often, our talents are so familiar to us that we don't even recognise them as talents in the first place. Recognising your talents and making a conscious decision to use them will be one of the best things that you could do in business. No business owner can be good at every area of their business. Smart business owners know this and know how to use their talents and delegate the rest. Finding someone who is better than you is key to success, but trying to be good at everything all of the time will only exhaust you and ultimately lead to your demise.

4. Determination

The dictionary defines determination as *the ability to continue trying to do something, although it is very difficult.* So difficulty is an essential part of building a business; nothing worthwhile comes easily. Richard Branson said: "*The ability to tap into your determination and grit is not just an innate skill. You can teach yourself to get up every day and try to keep a new business going, despite long odds, partly by structuring your life and job to make sure you are working toward your larger goals.*"

"You just got to go play. And no matter how many times it knocks you down. No matter how many times you think you can't go forward. No matter how many times things just don't go right. You know, anybody can quit. Anybody can do that. A Hall of Famer never quits. A Hall of Famer realizes that,

a Hall of Famer realizes that the crime is not being knocked down, the crime is not getting up again."

- Lawrence Taylor

Business owners who succeed are those who have done the same thing for a long period of time – sometimes it is just that simple. Live, learn and try again until you succeed. Great businesses owners never give up, they never give in.

It was Winston Churchill who simply said, *"Never, never, never give up."*

5. Education

Yes, education is important, but not the type of education that you might assume is important. I have little formal education. Pregnant at 17 years old, I found my way in life without even a high school diploma. Fortunately, my first husband's step grandparents were extremely wealthy and they gave us a roof over our heads when we were first married. Days were long and boring, and although I attempted to use the time to complete my high school diploma, I struggled. I was not an academic! However, I loved to read and I educated myself about all the subjects that interested me through reading.

Since that point until today, I can say that I have invested in educating myself about the things that matter to me. I have learned about parenting, being a wife, being a Christian, being a bookkeeper, and being a businesswoman through surrounding myself with the right people and reading the right books. To this day, I still do not have any pieces of paper to confirm my education, but I can confidently say that I have done all I can to educate myself in my specific areas of interest. My point is not that you don't need formal education or a university degree to get ahead in business, but rather that we can allow education to mean so much more than what it truly means in this day and age.

Chris Gardner offers words of wisdom in this area, saying, "If you don't take the necessary steps to make them happen, dreams are just mirages that mess with your head!" Education is learning, edification, or an enlightening experience. Allow yourself to be educated by anything and everything so that you can be the best version of you possible. Your business will only grow as you grow, so invest all you can in being more and educating yourself with necessary knowledge.

6. Character

Without great character, you will never succeed. Character is your moral fibre, your nature and your personal qualities. Poor character will lead to poor business and, on the flip side, excellent character will lead to excellent business. As Dee Hock, Founder and CEO of Emeritus VISA International, said: "*Control is not leadership; management is not leadership; leadership is leadership. If you seek to lead, invest at least 50 percent of your time leading yourself—your own purpose, ethics, principles, motivation, conduct.*" Henry David Thoreau, an American author, poet, philosopher, abolitionist, naturalist, tax resister, development critic, surveyor, and historian, said: "*You cannot dream yourself into a character; you must hammer and forge yourself one.*" And Abraham Lincoln said: "*Character is like a tree and reputation is like its shadow. The shadow is what we think of it; the tree is the real thing.*"

In a nutshell, character is something that you need and something that is acquired and developed intentionally. Without good character, your business is likely to fail sooner or later. Work consistently on developing your character. Allow adversity to sharpen who you are and refuse to compromise your integrity for just a quick "buck". Business owners with good character will earn loyalty and trust.

7. Purpose

Why are you in business? Punit Renjen, Chairman of the Board for Deloitte LLP, puts it this way: "*An organisation's culture of purpose answers the critical questions of who it is and why it exists. They have a culture of purpose beyond making a profit. An organisation's culture of purpose answers the critical questions of who we are and why we exist through a set of carefully articulated core beliefs. A culture of purpose guides behaviour, influences strategy, transcends leaders – and endures."*

So, as you can see, your "why" is a very important question to answer, and if your why is purely for money then it is not big enough. Why do you want to make money? Why do you get out of bed every day? Why do you do what you do? If the answers to these questions don't excite you, then change what you are doing. Richard Branson said, *"Most businesses fail, so if you're going to succeed, it has to be about more than making money."*

Here is Punit Renjen's blueprint for building a culture of purpose:

Articulate: Capture exactly who you are in language that's specific and clear. Write it down.

Propagate: Take the organisation's purpose that has been articulated, and communicate and illustrate it subtly and steadily over time.

Embed: Create the framework of programmes and operations that give your people a way to live the organisation's purpose.

Live: Align the behaviour of leaders and employees alike with "who you are" and "why you exist".

8.   Integrity

Phillip Brooks said, *"A man who lives right, and is right, has more power in his silence than another has by his words."*

You can build a business without integrity – many have – but you cannot sustain a business without integrity. At some point, a business owner with a lack of integrity will fall. Recently, I had the privilege of conducting business with a very well-known, very wealthy businessman. We worked very closely together on a sensitive project that attracted the attention of the international media. On a few occasions, we both found ourselves in difficult situations. Integrity is always revealed when the pressure is on, not in the easy times. Needless to say, I saw things in that businessman that shocked me. I couldn't believe the lack of integrity in him. Please understand, I am not saying this from a judgemental position as I too told a blatant lie to the press during one of these times of pressure and felt terribly guilty for doing so. I was very new in dealing with the press and have since learned some very important lessons; hopefully, if I found myself in the same situation once again, I would answer differently.

Nevertheless, I very quickly learned who I could trust out of the group of eight men that I was working with on this project. Some clearly had integrity and others clearly didn't. (I wonder what they would say about what they saw in me.) Integrity has always been one of my greatest desires and I constantly work hard at becoming a woman of integrity. Some men and women in business sadly don't value or desire integrity, and will do whatever it takes to make money, even if it involves dishonestly and unethically gaining it.

Growing Your Business With Integrity

Integrity is synonymous with trust. Being a person with integrity is a decision that you make and a line that you constantly evaluate, based on your own convictions. We all have room for improvement and should all do the best we can to walk with integrity. My own integrity is constantly challenged, as soon as I think I have integrity I stumble across yet another area that needs to be sharpened. I believe integrity is a journey you choose to go on and a lifestyle you choose to lead. No one is born with it but we all have the choice to work on it. Here are some simple tips to grow your business with integrity:

- **Be reliable**; do what you say you are going to do.
- **Be consistent** in your ethos and standards.
- **Be positive**; it makes people feel good.

- **Be kind**; treat people well.
- **Be honest**; don't lie or cheat under any circumstances.

So there you have it – it really *is* possible to build a successful business from scratch with next to nothing. And no amount of capital can compensate for having the core characteristics needed to be a successful entrepreneur. Do you have all these characteristics? Do you have some, and not others? Work on all these characteristics and you will soon see a drastic difference in your business!

I Did it With Children

> "Life is 10% what happens to me and 90% how I react to it."
>
> - Charles R. Swindoll

Children, our greatest educators!

o you see your children as a distraction from your work or your work as a distraction from your children? Or are you simply one of those people that use your children as an excuse for not doing anything significant? I often hear women say, *"I can't"* and then list an excuse that is connected to their children, fully expecting understanding and sympathy as a result. Or perhaps they expect a medal for being the world's greatest mum because they gave up everything to be on 24-hour call for their children. I have four children and I have got a lot right and a lot wrong as a mother! There is no such thing as a perfect mother; we will all make mistakes along the way. The greatest gift you can give your children is to be authentic and lead by example. Children copy. They will copy your good habits and your bad habits. If they are not intentionally raised well at home then they will just copy anyone else who comes along. Don't fear living your life because you don't want to let your children down. Live your life as best you can so that they have something worthwhile to copy and to look up to. There is no right way to raise a child because every single child is different and every single adult is different. Raise your children according to your convictions.

When my eldest two were in their pre-school years, I was a stay at home mum. We had very little money and I was perfectly content. I loved staying home, playing house and mummy. Looking back, I can also see that I was a very young mother who lacked confidence, had no formal education, and did not realise how much of "me" was still undiscovered. Over the years, my natural skill slowly emerged, and opportunities to work part time came up as a result. It was a very natural process and, by the time my two daughters were settled at school, I was ready to do something else with my time. My conviction was to be a mother first and I harshly judged working mothers as I could not understand how they could leave their precious little ones to go to work. In my eyes, I would rather be poor and happy than sacrifice my family just for a little extra money. My conviction at the time was that all mothers should stay home with their children. It suited me and I firmly believed I was right.

Many years and another husband later, I found myself pregnant, and I was thrilled to get a chance to go through the whole baby stage again. My circumstances were vastly different at this stage of my life and I did not stop working on my own business, not even for one day when my third child, my son Daniel, was born. I distinctly remember breastfeeding at the computer regularly and, when he was a little older, I would split the computer screen in half so I could work on one half and he could watch the animal alphabet on the other half. At times, I felt guilty, but most of the time I was content with our lifestyle. By the time our fourth little princess came along, I was an established businesswoman and public speaker. Amy was born on Saturday and on Sunday I was back home, cleaning the house and checking emails. My work was very important to me and I was sure that as long as I kept the balance right, everything would be alright. I didn't stop working after my youngest two children were born and felt that it was acceptable as I worked from home, so could juggle everything that I wanted to do in my day. It dawned on me that I had been horribly judgemental of working mothers when I was younger and realised that, although being a stay home mum was right for me at the time, it wasn't the only right way. However, I still very harshly judged mothers who dumped their children at day care so they could go to work. I thought that it was simply too much and children deserved better. I looked down on mothers who did this just for a bit of extra income and felt justified by my lifestyle as my children still had access to me whenever they needed me. I was the multi-tasking queen and could do a variety of different things at the same time!

Ashamedly, I look back over my life and realise that there is no right way. Each woman must decide for herself what is important to her and make the necessary sacrifices accordingly. We only get one life so we should live it in a way that we feel is best. I look back now at how harsh and critical I was of other women, only to realise that it was my own insecurities of not being enough that I was projecting onto them. If they were wrong then I could feel better about myself. Of course, they were not wrong; they were just doing what they perceived to be best and right for their own life. Today, I do my best to see things as impartially as possible. I also try to mind my own business and not compare myself with anyone else, as it is just bad character to do so.

My favourite thing to do is work from home in my little home office with my door shut! My children understand that when the door is shut, I should not be disturbed; when it is slightly ajar, they may come in if it is important, and if the door is wide open, they may hang out in my office with me. I can't say this is the right way to do it for everyone but it is my way and it works for me. I know of some women that absolutely can't stand working from home and are happy to pay extra for an office away from home and day care for their children just so that they can work in an environment that stimulates them.

Is either right or wrong? Of course not! We all have to find what works best for us. The most important thing is that we have balance and give our children the love and care that they need. In our home, we have a family day once a week that is only for family time and activities, and we have extra special time at bedtime during the week. Our children know that when we are working not to bother us (my husband works from home too), but when it is their time, they are allowed to "demand" our full attention. If I am on my phone or laptop during family time, I get in a lot of trouble with my six year old, Amy. So that's how we do it and it works perfectly for us. What lifestyle makes you and your family happy? That is the most important question that needs answering. It doesn't matter what anyone else thinks or says about it, *you* have to be content with how you raise your children and how you choose to do it is up to you and what works best for you and your family.

"Be who you are and say what you feel because those who mind don't matter and those who matter don't mind."

- Dr. Seuss

The work life balance is one that many women have spent decades trying to figure out and, more recently, we see many men facing the same challenge. I used to be very black and white in these matters, as you no doubt can tell, with clearly defined roles in my mind, both for men and women. I lived my life according to these "boxes" and judged those that dared to live a life different to what I perceived to be right. That was until my whole world was turned upside down and now it doesn't resemble anything close to what I perceived to be right! My husband does the school run, I am starting to work out of town a lot, we share the cleaning and cooking, and as for the rest, we juggle and make it work. I never in my wildest dreams imagined that my life would be like this and, guess what... it's great! Although I do understand my husband's need for a *womanly* wife and I understand his need to be the king of his castle, we are both comfortable making our life together work, no matter what it takes. Our four children are thrown into the mix, along with our two cats, Muffin and Poppy. We are one big, happy, slightly unusual and very crazy family – and we are all very happy most days!

There *Are* Enough Hours in the Day

You are in control of your schedule; your schedule does not control you. If you feel that there aren't enough hours in the day then it is up to you to make your hours work better for you. Choice is powerful but too many business owners forget to use it. You don't have to take every call, you don't have to check every social media site every day, you don't have to check your email every day, and you certainly don't need to work from 6am to midnight every night. It's your choice and it's your life. We all get 24 hours each and every day, but some use them wisely and others don't. There is no perfect work life balance. Life is messy and chaotic, and each and every day will look different from the previous one, no matter how hard you try. My best advice is to love the life you have each day that you have it, with no regrets for what you did or didn't do that day.

Some days I get it wrong; I overwork and get tense with my children or just end up in a heap crying! I wake up the next day and try again. Most days I get it right. Interestingly enough, I have never said that I have spent too much time with my children or my husband on any of my days. I also don't end up tense after spending time with them as I would if I overworked. So what is the interruption then? Is my work the interruption to my family and quality of life or is my family the interruption to my work? This is a question you must answer for yourself.

Learn From Your Children

Did you know that your children can be a great source of inspiration and creative ideas in your business? No matter what the age they are, you can learn a great deal from them.

Ask them questions.

One great question you can ask your child is what they think you do in your business. Their answer could be amusing or it could give you a clue as to how other people perceive your business. You could also ask them questions, such as what colour should I use, and why or how would you run my business. Some answers will simply be entertaining and lighten the mood of your day, but others may get you to think outside the box. Most importantly, chatting with your children about your business is a great way to make them feel involved and important.

Ask their opinion.

A more specific question you could ask your children is their opinion on a certain matter. If they say that they don't understand what you are asking then try again until they do understand. Communication is essential in business, and if you can communicate something well to a child then you know you have cracked it! Sometimes I even ask my children what to wear or how I look with a particular hairstyle or outfit – they always respond honestly!

Ask them to solve a problem.

Another great thing you can do is to give a business problem to your children to solve but tell them it is a game. Of course, there are problems that simply won't be suitable for children to solve, depending on the type of business you run, but don't underestimate them; you may be pleasantly surprised at what they come up with.

Include them on the journey.

Learning from our children also allows them to learn from us. Including them on your business journey can only have a positive impact on them. As there is so much to learn and discover, why not start them off young? Don't you wish that you got to *play* business a lot earlier on in life? I certainly do. I do recall playing shop which I love to play now as a grownup too. I also loved to work with money as a child and still love to balance the books now. There is a lot to be said for play, our children could be *playing* their future career right now.

Teach them business principles.

Principles are principles and can be taught and learned by anyone. Taking the time to teach your children basic business principles will also help you get real clarity on them too. Sometimes we forget the importance of the basics but teaching and playing the basics with our children will not only help them, it will help us too.

On one occasion, I gave my youngest children (five and seven years old at the time) £20 and told them that it was capital for that entire year. It was up to them to make it grow, as I would not be giving them any more money for that year. We had great fun creating in and out columns for their money, and then brainstorming ideas to make their money grow. We all had a great time and I was slowly able to teach them some basic principles that would serve them well in life. Daniel is a brilliant writer, even at the tender age of seven, so he decided to write a book of poems to sell. This led him to start his own blog too, which he could later monetise if his poems took off. At the moment, it is full of monster and dinosaur pictures and a few poems; we are still working on the actual making the money grow part!

I did this same exercise with my other two daughters several years prior and one of them invested their money by buying a set of birds to breed. Sadly, we ended up confiscating the birds and giving them away as she seldom fed them or gave them water. It was a great idea but it didn't work. It turned out that she first needed to learn a few other lessons before she could make her money grow with live animals. I am pleased to report that she is doing much better with money now and does not own any birds. Trusting children with pets as an investment opportunity is not the wisest thing to do without supervision at all times.

A Seven Year Old Millionaire

The point is not to make an instant millionaire or to avoid any sort of failure. It is about teaching them valuable principles, helping them learn from their mistakes, and enjoying the journey along the way. Even teaching them to learn to deal with failure will help them through the harsh reality of life, no matter what career or business they end up choosing. In the end, they (and you) will be better off for it and hopefully a lot closer as a family too.

Top Tips for Juggling Children at Home

Breathe

Oh, how many of life's problems would be solved if we just took the time to take a deep breath? Before getting annoyed with your children because they are bothering you again, breathe in deeply and out again slowly, and then respond. If necessary, do it twice before responding. Most of the time, you will find your anger turns into love and, instead of shouting at them, you will hug them and ask them what they need. It usually only takes five minutes to hear what a child needs anyway, and if you are smart, you will train them from young to make their own snacks and sandwiches so that rather than having to pause to make food, you can simply say, "Yes, of course you may" when they ask for food. This shouldn't be applied to dinner, of course, unless they are over 16 and have learned to cook!

Eat

There is a great Zen proverb: "*When walking, walk. When eating, eat.*" Do you stop work to eat? Are your children at home at lunch or dinner time? Why not focus on eating together when it is time to eat? No phones or computers at the table. If it's warm, eat outside in the garden. Make eating a quality part of your life rather than something you do hurriedly whilst working. If you chat to your children over a meal, they will feel satisfied that they have had some attention, leaving you to get on with work.

Sleep

I don't know about you but I am a terrible mother when I am sleep deprived! My patience wears thin and even my hearing seems to go and I have to ask my children to repeat themselves a thousand times, especially first thing in the morning after too little sleep. Sleep is important! It is not something we can do less of to save time, or something we can neglect because we are too busy. I could write a whole separate book on the importance of sleep, and will touch on it more in the next chapter. Don't compromise on sleep – it is not worth it and, not only will it damage your family life, but it will also damage the potential of your business in the long run.

Exercise

Endorphins are essential for working mums! Get them as often as possible. Exercise is great for getting rid of stress and for producing endorphins. You can incorporate exercise with family time, but if you really want the maximum benefits, take time to exercise alone, three or four times a week minimum. You will be a better mother and a better businesswoman if you incorporate exercise into your routine. Once again, I will go into this in greater detail in the next chapter.

Play

All work and no play is pointless! What is life for but to enjoy? Even if we enjoy our work, we still need an element of play; it is good for you on so many levels. Play board games with your children, play hide and seek, play in the park, tell jokes and generally be playful. It's good for them and good for you too.

"We don't stop playing because we grow old; we grow old because we stop playing."

- George Bernard Shaw

Play fuels your imagination, improves your mood, enhances problem-solving skills, and generally improves your mental health. Actively playing with your children will make your children brighter, better adjusted, and less anxious.

If you work at home with a young child, have a box of activities that they can play with on their own while you are working. Teach them to have time to play on their own, as well as time to play with you. Just remember, they will be sitting at your feet for such a short length of time. Don't push yourself too hard when you have little ones – enjoy your precious time with them because, before you know it, they will be grown up and will have moved out.

Be More With Less

Ditch multi-tasking and truly be present in each and every moment. When working, work. When playing with your children, play. When cleaning, clean. By embracing each moment, you get so much more pleasure out of life, no matter what you are doing. I remember a time when I found ironing fun. I would turn my music up loud and work through a pile of ironing while singing along to my favourite tunes. It was a peaceful time and thinking about it again reminds me of the peace I once had.

Today, ironing is a joke! However, I have introduced a few solutions to manage it. I usually wrinkle test clothes before buying them so I don't have to iron anything. Hanging up the laundry in a particular way and folding it perfectly also eliminates ironing. As you can no doubt tell, I seldom iron, and when I do, it is either my trousers with my hair straighteners because I am in a hurry or my husband's shirt, if he is lucky. What happened to that carefree, peaceful little housewife that I once was? Back then, I had no money, a humble rented house, and a little baby girl. Life was simple and I remember being very happy. Somewhere between then and now, I got BUSY but made a lot of money doing so! To be perfectly honest, I can't say I am any happier for it. Back then, I was ignorant and ignorance was bliss. Now I know a lot more, run a successful company, and am trying to enjoy my journey without compromising the peace and joy that I had when I was a little less busy. I don't see the point of swapping one for the other – it doesn't need to be success or peace and joy – it can be and should always be both!

My journey has been wonderful. I have learned much and figured out what really matters in life. Most importantly, I have learned that I can decide how busy I get. I am not a victim to modern day living but a ruler over my lifestyle. My determination to find the balance is not only for my own pleasure but also so that I can model it to my children. The more I give up and the less busy I become, the more I get back to living this incredible life to the full.

"Dream as if you will live forever; live as if you will die today."

- James Dean

Carpe Diem

Carpe diem is another great key for living. It is a Latin saying, usually translated as "seize the day", taken from a poem in the Odes in 23 BC by the poet, Horace. This phrase is actually a part of the longer *"Carpe diem quam minimum credula postero"*, which translates into *"Seize the day, putting as little trust as possible in the next (day)"*.

All we have is this second, and at any point in any day, it can all end. Jesus Christ said, *"Therefore do not worry about tomorrow, for tomorrow will worry about itself. Each day has enough trouble of its own."* Why waste our precious life with worry when we could simply live each day as if it were our last and really truly live? On our deathbed, will we regret the money we didn't get to make or the time we missed out on with our children while we were so busy making money? I can assure you it will be the latter. Life is a journey, not a destination, but too often we are so focused on what we perceive to be the destination and we miss out on life itself. Carpe diem and teach your children to carpe diem too! As William Wallace in Mel Gibson's *Braveheart* said, *"Every man dies. Not every man really lives."*

How to Carpe Diem:

Wake up early

Starting the day early can have a great effect on your productivity and enjoyment of the day. Some professions don't allow for a nice, comfortable overnight sleep and early rise but most do. Several studies have even linked waking up early with business success. Christoph Randler, a Harvard biologist, also discovered that early risers are more proactive. Waking up early helps you to have time to get organised for the day, time to exercise, time to pray or meditate, time in silence to focus your mind, and it can also just give you some time to yourself, if that is what you need. To really seize the day, seize it early. Children naturally wake up early so it needs to be earlier than your children too! Of course, if you have little ones and value every second of sleep, you can allocate yourself a little time mid morning while they are napping or at another convenient moment. When my eldest daughter was a baby, my time alone was lunch time, during her two hour nap. When my youngest was a baby, my time was in the morning before she woke up as she slept later than the others. It's all about finding what works for your current situation.

Eat the frog first

Mark Twain offered some fantastic advice when he said, *"Eat a live frog first thing in the morning and nothing worse will happen to you the rest of the day."* I sincerely hope he didn't literally eat a frog, yuck! Nevertheless, the principle is fantastic; to truly get the most out of the day, do the task that you are least looking forward to first. That way the rest of the day is free to do what you enjoy doing. I have wasted too many days procrastinating and have learned just to get on with the things I don't want to do but have to, so I don't waste my precious days.

"The best way to get something done is to begin."

- Author Unknown

What are you putting off right now that you know is wasting your precious time? I challenge you to put this book down right now and go do it, then come back and continue reading! Why not? Just get it done or started and get it out of the way. You will feel so much better for it.

Learn something new

Try to learn something new every day! Your brain is a muscle and, if you want to keep it functioning well, you need to use it. As we get older, we become content with what we already know, and perhaps even complacent. Remind yourself to soak up all you can every day. There is always something new to learn and it can be very enjoyable. I am currently learning to play the guitar. Most days I make time to sit with my guitar, sing some of my favourite songs and try to play along. It's really fun, a great stress relief, and quite satisfying to be learning something new. Next I would like to learn to paint and take up Pilates. There is so much to do and learn that one lifetime just doesn't seem like enough time! I read a lot to learn more about leadership and business, and I also read fiction to give my brain a break as it is always ON. As a family, we also play board games, but try to play the ones that we can learn from, such as Scrabble, Bug Bingo (my son's favourite – I have learned loads of new bug names already), and even Monopoly, so we can teach our children about money and property.

Teach your children to love to learn too. You could even make it a daily conversation point or game. Recently, I read that learning helps us more easily and readily adapt to new situations, and that learning makes us more confident.

Take risks

Life is too short to play it safe all the time. Too many business owners play it safe for fear of failure, but life's best lessons and greatest rewards come from failure. Even in life and love, take risks and live a little. I learned not to hold back too much by asking myself – what is the worst that can happen? Once I have established the worst case scenario in my mind, I am free to take the leap! Ask your children the same question too when they are scared to take a risk or do something scary. On the flip side, of course, teach them about calculating the risk and not just jumping blindly into everything. As with all things in this life, balance is essential. There are calculated risks where you are happy to suffer the worst that can happen if needs be but there are stupid risks where you risk more than you are willing to lose.

Welcome new experiences

My husband has been very guilty of not welcoming new experiences in the past. Many times, I would suggest a new experience for us and he would decline, based on the assumption that he wouldn't like it. Our son has picked up the same habit, but our daughters like to try all sorts of things, just like me. It's taken years of pushing and pulling and proving my case to get our family on the same page with this one! I remember the first time I invited my husband ice-skating for our date night. He protested, saying that he didn't like ice-skating. When I asked if he had ever tried it, he said no. So, of course, my immediate response was, "Well how do you know that you don't like it then?!" I eventually convinced him to try and I am not pleased to report that he only went around the rink once and decided that he didn't like it! The rest of the date night consisted of me ice-skating and him watching until we both got bored enough to admit defeat. I am still not convinced that he doesn't like ice-skating because he didn't give it a fair go! This is one of *many* examples and, most of the time, he ends up enjoying the new activity that I propose. Today, based on very many positive past experiences, he is less reluctant to try new things now. Try new things individually and as a family; you might love it, you might hate it, but at least you explored something new together! Further down the line, you will treasure the memory either way.

Many giggles come from failed experiments or what was a disaster at the time. I remember a time when we first moved to Cheltenham and were exploring the nearby Leckhampton Hill. I bravely started my way up a steep cliff face, as I love climbing and exploring. The only thing was that it was lime stone and I am used to the South African solid rocks that don't crumble in your hands when you grab onto them. As I neared the top, the areas that I gripped onto began to crumble. I looked down. It was a steep drop. Fear gripped me as I imagined the worst. I cried out for help and sobbed like a little girl, paralysed with fear as the children watched their silly mother stuck to the side of a small cliff. Eric ran to the top of the cliff from a different angle and gallantly came to my rescue by pulling me up to a place of safety. To this day, we laugh about that experience. At the time, it was terrifying, but it certainly created a memory and a story that will be told for years to come... at my expense, of course! The point is that I tried something – it didn't work out, I will never do it again – but it was worth it as it is one of our memories.

Be amazed by things

My second eldest daughter, Jordan, finds me embarrassing. She says I am too passionate about every tiny, little thing. When we go for walks, I marvel at the tiniest flower or the unusual moss hanging from a tree. I suddenly stand frozen to attention when I notice a bird. What she particularly dislikes is when I spontaneously burst into song in a public place because I am happy. On these occasions, when walking with Jordan and her eldest sister, Lorah, one will move over to the other side of the street and the other will sing along. How different the two of them are!

Nevertheless, I am easily amazed by things and love to marvel at the world around me. It was only when I went back to London, after living in Cheltenham for a few years, that I realised what an amazing city it is. Going back for a visit, as opposed to walking through the city to and from work, allowed me to appreciate it so much more than I did when I was running around in the rat race. I wonder if my working days would have been far more productive and enjoyable if I took the walk to work a little slower and marvelled at the world around me as I went about my business. Are you marvelling at things or simply rushing from one thing to the next each day? Take time to be amazed by people too. We seldom appreciate those around us and taking time to do so will not only have a positive impact on our life but on their lives too.

Don't put off until tomorrow

Benjamin Franklin, Philip Stanhope, Thomas Jefferson, Charles Dickens, Napoleon Hill and many more all agreed on one thing by saying, "*Don't put off until tomorrow what you can do today*". Putting things off is procrastination and, as Benjamin Franklin said, "*You may delay, but time will not, and lost time is never found again.*" Charles Dickens quite aptly said, "*Procrastination is the thief of time.*"

We procrastinate with things we don't want to do, such as tax returns, emptying the bin, or making a list of phone calls for our business, but we also procrastinate about the important things, such as reading that bedtime story, baking that cake with the children, or going to the park. If you know you should be doing something, do it then and there! Don't wait; don't put it off because you may end up never doing it. Make little memories with your children every day, rather than waiting for that one big memory that you plan to make in the future that never comes. If reading a bedtime story is being put off, why not start with just two pages a night? If you don't find time to bake that cake then why not buy a dozen readymade cupcakes from the shop and ice them together with homemade icing? Rather than continually putting things off, find a small step in the right direction to get started today. This principle can apply to most areas of procrastination. For example, make two phone calls a day, rather than waiting for a moment to sit down and make 20. Jog around the block twice a week, rather than waiting until you can run a marathon. I don't know how you will deal with the bin slowly; if it is full, just empty it!

Give your best to whatever you do

Nothing is worth doing if you don't do it well. At the Women's Business Club, we always say that if we can't do it well, we won't do it at all. The same goes for our family life. Don't raise your children on your scraps of time and energy. Give them your best; make a real effort to engage with them on many levels. When spending time with them, *be* with them 100 per cent. Colour in with all your heart, bake that cake with passion, play Frisbee in the park like you mean it, and cuddle and love like there is no tomorrow. If you can't do it well, set aside a time when you can (but don't procrastinate!). Your children deserve the best of you.

I Did it With Depression

"When fate hands you a lemon, make lemonade."

- Dale Carnegie

What you believe, you become.

The truth is that one of the reasons for me doing "it" in my pyjamas was because there were days when getting out of bed was a real challenge. It's not that I was lazy and slept late – quite the contrary – I actually struggled to sleep much at all. Depression has been a huge challenge and, some days, getting up and getting dressed would be almost impossible. So I tricked myself some days by bypassing the dressing stage and simply working in my pyjamas, at times even in bed. Somehow, this helped. Somehow, not having to get dressed, put makeup on, brush my hair, brush my teeth, eat breakfast, etc. helped me have the energy to turn my laptop on and deal with the day ahead. Some days I would work in my pyjamas in bed all day and deal with all the admin bits and bobs. Other days, I would make it to my office and conduct a full day of work in my pyjamas. Most days I was fine. I would get up, get dressed and get out into the real world and have a great time. However, the reason I managed to do so well on those days was because I cut myself some slack on the *other* days; the days that were a little bit more difficult.

Life happens. Good things happen and bad things happen to everyone! It's what you do with what happens that counts. I struggle with depression. My hormonal cycle is the same as every other woman's, which means I get very grumpy days. Some days I wake up and feel ugly. I don't like emptying the bin or making sandwiches for my children. I have difficulty sleeping. Dirty cat litter trays make me retch. My skin is terrible and I am prone to acne, even at 41 years old.

OK, that's enough about me, what about you? What do you struggle with, dislike, or have to put up with in your life? Is your life perfect right now?

Of course not! Are you waiting for life to be better before you do something with it? I hope not! You can start building a successful business right this minute with the current circumstances that life has thrown at you, and with exactly the resources that you have available to you right now. Can you see it? Do you believe me? If you answered no to either of these questions then that is where your problem lies, not in your current situation. If all I could see was myself depressed then all I would ever be is depressed. Seeing past the depression and onto a bright, successful future is an essential part of my journey. Does that mean that my depression will go? I honestly don't know. My hope and vision of myself is one without depression, but even if it stays, I will still build the life I dream of and enjoy every part of the journey. What I have decided to do is to find a way to get on with life, despite depression. Depression doesn't define me or determine my future; it is merely something that I have, just like I have bad skin. I continue to fight depression and I continue to try new remedies for my skin. So far so good.

Understanding You

My first real step forward from depression was realising that I had depression and learning how to deal with it. Most importantly, I decided not to use it as an excuse to stay home and feel sorry for myself, but I found keys to living a full life, knowing that I had this handicap. Do you have something in your life right now that you are using as an excuse not to lead a full life? It may not be depression but are you using your children as an excuse, or your husband or wife? Perhaps you didn't finish high school. Is that your excuse, or do you have a physical handicap you hide behind? The list could go on and on. Excuses are easy to come by; every single person in the world has something that they can justify as an excuse not to build a great life. The key is not the handicap but the belief around it.

What you believe, you become. As Abraham Lincoln quite rightly said, "*We can be as happy as we make up our minds to be.*" If you believe you cannot do it, whatever "it" is, guess what? You will not be able to do it. You will find it even more of a challenge if you are verbalising your negative belief. Your ears hear what you are saying, your heart believes it, and your head causes you to act accordingly. It is a simple yet complex process. The simple part is how to influence it through your thoughts. The complex part is what happens as a result of your thoughts. Your underlying beliefs create your thoughts, thoughts become actions, actions become habits, and habits turn into a lifestyle.

"Your underlying beliefs create your thoughts, thoughts become actions, actions become habits, and habits turn into a lifestyle."

Changing your life is as simple as changing your beliefs. If I believed that I was depressed and could not build a successful national company then I would never have achieved what I have achieved so far. I would be at home crying most days! However, I believe that I am a very successful businesswoman and have created a lifestyle that results from this belief. Crying days still exist but rarely, and they do not define me. So what if I work in my pyjamas some days – does it really matter?

I understand myself and my limitations. Being an introvert means that people drain me. Too many days out with people could wipe me out completely. Working in my pyjamas at least once a week means that I cope better and keep the balance in my life. I allow myself to have these days so that when I am out with people networking, presenting, encouraging, giving, giving, giving, I can give from a place of strength. If I didn't allow myself "down days" then I would be mediocre on my days out with people. If you are an introvert, you will completely understand what I am talking about, and if you are not, you will be scratching your head right now thinking that I am loopy, so let me flip the coin for you extroverts.

Extroverts need to be around people. They get their energy from others and are often drained from too much time alone. Place an extrovert in a situation where they are stuck in an office or a room all day, every day alone and they will become drained, just like an introvert is drained by too much people contact. If an extrovert works from home, they need to ensure that they plan enough time with people to stay fresh and inspired. If an introvert works from home, they have to ensure that they plan enough time with people so that they don't become complete hermits. It's all about understanding yourself and creating a lifestyle and "work style" based on that understanding. I have spent many years learning about who I am and, today, I find that all those years was time well invested, as this knowledge gives me an edge and freedom to get on with living.

The UK Office for National Statistics released a report measuring national well-being in 2012, and found the following in the area of mental health:

"Mental health and well-being are fundamental to quality of life, enabling people to experience life as meaningful and to be creative and active citizens. Mental health is an essential component of social cohesion, productivity and peace and stability in the living environment, contributing to social capital and economic development in societies (WHO, 2005). Positive mental health can be described as people thinking and feeling good about themselves, and feeling able to cope with their problems. This positivity is important to an individual's well-being. Mental health differs from mental illness. Mental illness covers a range of mental health problems, which can cause marked emotional distress and interfere with daily function, including different types of depression and anxiety. These types of problems can also have a detrimental effect on an individual's well-being."

So, it is plain to see that I am not alone. There is a high percentage of people who also suffer with depression in the UK, and I am sure the numbers would be similar in the USA and other countries. Paul Farmer, Chief Executive of Mind, the UK's leading mental health charity, said: *"Too often people don't speak up, fearing a negative response, which means they don't get access to timely support."* The former chairman of HBOS, Lord

Stevenson, who spoke openly about his experiences with depression, said: *"There was no apparent reason for it, everything in my life was lovely."* In *The Wall Street Journal*, Tufts University psychiatry professor Nassir Ghaemi was quoted from his book, *A First-Rate Madness: Uncovering the Links Between Leadership and Mental Illness*, as saying, *"In times of crisis and tumult, those who are mentally abnormal, even ill, become the greatest leaders. We might call this the Inverse Law of Sanity."*

It is my choice to either believe that depression is a handicap and I cannot be all I can be as a result, or I can believe that it could be one of the things that makes me a better businesswoman and leader. The great thing is that what I believe, I become, so I choose to believe that it will be to my advantage. All I have to do is learn how to use it and cope with it. One day, I may not have depression anymore, or I may never overcome it, I honestly don't know, but I am not going to wait to find out – my life goes on.

"I have a dream..."

- Martin Luther King Jr

Reverend Dr. Martin Luther King Jr., one of the most significant Americans of the 20th century, attempted suicide at 12 years old by jumping from a second-storey window in his family home after the death of his grandmother. He had multiple periods of severe depression all through his life and, in his later years, some of his staff tried to persuade him to get psychiatric treatment, but he refused. History as we know it would be significantly different if this great man allowed his depression to determine his outcome. He had a dream and focused on the dream, as opposed to focusing on the handicap. What do you focus on, the dream or the handicap?

Here follows a lovely article written by Bex Cobham, one of our members in the Forest of Dean Women's Business Club:

It's time to talk about mental health in business. Mental health issues affect people from all walks of life. In fact, the mental health charity, Mind, say that 1 in 4 people will experience mental health issues each year. So, why is there still stigma surrounding the issue?

Employers have a duty of care towards their employees, but what happens when you're the business owner?

Employment law in the UK states that an employer has a duty of care towards their staff when it comes to providing health, safety and welfare for all their employees (Health and Safety at Work Act 1984), and this includes their mental health and welfare.

What happens when you're a sole trader or a small business owner and you run into difficulties? Well, unfortunately the buck stops with you, because you're the one responsible for seeing to your own mental health and welfare.

Networking: not just for generating sales

Now, we all know that networking is great for your business. We're told time and time again to get out there and generate leads – and sales. However, we at the Women's Business Club also recognise that the group plays a crucial role in providing less tangible benefits that are of equal importance. Chief amongst these is support! Whether it's a business or personal matter, the Women's Business Club believes in offering this support, because we want to see our members succeed.

1 in 4 people will suffer from a mental illness each year

Yes, there's still an aura of stigma and ignorance surrounding mental illness, but there really needn't be. Next time you're at an event, it's statistically likely that around 1 in 4 of those people nearby you are currently dealing with a mental illness of some kind!

In fact, a member of the Women's Business Club recently spoke out about her 18 month battle with depression. Should she have been so candid? Well, it sparked a discussion where other members came forth and offered their support. This, in turn, led to further discussion between members about their own struggles with depression, anxiety, PTSD (Post Traumatic Stress Disorder), Bipolar Disorder and more.

Are people scared of "catching mad"?

So, given the fact that so many people have dealt with mental health issues at one time or another, I started pondering the reasons why the stigma behind mental illness still endures.

- *First of all, I wondered whether people may be subconsciously afraid of "catching mad".*
- *Then there's the way that mentally ill people are sensationalised in the media and portrayed in television and film. After all, it's all about entertainment and giving people a gripping story, isn't it?*
- *Then there's just plain ignorance. If you've never experienced any mental health difficulties or don't know anyone who has (which is statistically unlikely), why should you have any knowledge of it?*
- *From a purely pragmatic viewpoint, is it a good idea to do business with someone you know who suffers from a mental illness? Can you rely on them?*

Why does the stigma endure? Let's talk about it!

Naturally, we want to do business with people who we can relate to easily, form good relationships with and trust. Nevertheless, people aren't machines! We can never know what physical health issues may be hiding around the corner, or predict earth-shattering, major life events that can and do come out of the blue. Anyone could potentially develop a mental health problem for all sorts of reasons.

Supporting each other

In fact, as business owners, we have to be particularly kind to ourselves as it's a stressful lifestyle – however rewarding it may be. People burn out, break down and crack under pressure – even CEOs of large organisations! So, it makes perfect sense to be candid when it comes to talking about your mental health issues as a business owner! We need to stick together and support other business owners.

Opening up can sound scary, but it could boost your productivity in the long term.

Fortunately, we at the Women's Business Club are an inclusive and supportive group. We don't judge people for being depressed or anxious – we all have issues of some kind that could potentially affect our business. Perhaps women are more likely to open up about this, rather than admit to a perceived weakness.

In fact, recent statistics were released on suicide rates, and men over 40 are now the highest risk group. So, why is this relevant to this post? Well, there's a number of reasons, but they are just less likely to talk about the problems they're facing. After all, we've been conditioned to see women as more open and communicative when it comes to discussing emotional matters with each other.

You'd be surprised by how many people have overcome these obstacles.

So, it's absolutely essential for people to be able to open up and talk about mental health issues – it saves lives. It's not something to be frightened of, and you'd be surprised by the number of strong and competent individuals who'll admit to having been through the ringer themselves!

Business owners have a lot to juggle!

In many ways, it's especially important for women in business to be able to talk to each other when they're feeling shaky. In spite of the feminists of the 1960s, we're still more likely to take on the lion's share of responsibilities when it comes to caring for children, family members and elderly relatives – and that's before we even consider our businesses and caring for ourselves.

Tips for Doing Business with Depression

Although I am focusing mainly on business, these tips apply to life in general too. Depression can affect our relationships, our businesses, our happiness, and so much of life. If you are a fellow sufferer, take back your life one step at a time. Depression is not the only thief of a full life if left unchecked; apply what you can to your situation from the tips below too as they can help with many of the things that have the potential to hold us back in life.

Sleep
We have touched on this subject already but it is also relevant to this area of mental health. Did you know that 65% of people are sleep deprived? Here are some interesting facts about sleep you probably did not know or were too tired to think about:

- Lack of sleep can cause cognitive and behavioural changes, including moodiness, concentration problems, paranoia, and hallucinations.
- Humans spend about 25 years of their life sleeping.
- Humans are the only mammals that willingly delay sleep.
- Body temperature and the brain's sleep cycle are closely linked, so either being too hot or too cold can affect your sleep.
- Staying awake for 17 hours leads to a decrease in performance equivalent to a blood alcohol-level of 0.05%.
- Sleeping pills can disrupt grieving.
- You can lose weight from sleeping! People who are sleep deprived are more likely to have bigger appetites the following day. Leptin (an

appetite-regulating hormone) levels fall when you don't get enough sleep.

- Do you sleep with your phone next to your bed? The smallest light, such as that that is emitted from a mobile phone blinking when a message is received, can be enough to disrupt the sleep cycle.

- Several studies suggest that women need up to an hour's extra sleep a night, compared to men. Not getting it may be one reason why women are more susceptible to depression than men.

The list could go on and on, but the bottom line is that sleep is essential for a healthy life. Sleeplessness has its most dramatic effect on the brain, which is why you can feel grumpy and moody from lack of sleep, as well as unable to think clearly and make wise decisions. Chronic sleep deprivation may lead to mental illness, obesity, heart disease, and so many more health conditions.

Most adults need around eight hours of sleep a night, some a little more and others a little less, but eight hours is a good guideline. Studies have shown that people who get a good night's sleep on a regular basis tend to live longer and healthier lives than those who sleep too few or too many hours each night.

Sleep and depression are closely linked. Depression may cause sleep problems but sleep problems may also contribute to depression. R. Robert Auger, MD, a sleep specialist at the Mayo Center, USA, said: *"If you were to follow people with insomnia and no history of depression, they would be four times more likely to develop depression than individuals with no history of insomnia."* Auger goes on to say, *"Sleep is as important an aspect of health as exercise and nutrition. Sleep is non-negotiable."*

Getting a good night's sleep is not optional for anyone, especially if you are prone to depression. Take sleep seriously. Make sure you work on your sleep pattern as you would on your business. It will have a direct effect on your business so, in a very real and practical way, you are actually working on your business by taking care of your sleep!

Eat

Food has a significant impact on mental health too and, in some cases, you can eat yourself well. Andrew McCulloch, the Chief Executive at the Mental Health Foundation, said: "*Diet is one of the important factors for our mental health.*" One thing I have learned in all my years of experimenting with food and depression treatments is that maintaining a constant blood sugar level is very important to healthy living. Simple things, such as reducing or cutting out sugar, alcohol and caffeine from your diet, can help keep your mood stable, reduce the production of stress hormones, and make us less tired or irritable.

Margaret Edwards of the mental health charity, SANE, said: "*Physical and mental health are closely related.*" Dr Eric Brunner, one of the researchers from University College London, said: "*There seem to be various aspects of lifestyle, such as taking exercise, which also matters, but it appears that diet is playing an independent role.*" I am not a nutritionist and there are plenty of wonderful books, studies and professionals out there that address healthy eating. Over the years I have very much enjoyed learning and discovering the effects that food has on my body and mind. An amusing example of what I learned is not to have a full carbohydrate lunch at work as it made me sleepy all afternoon! However, my personal research and experience has found that there are some foods that should definitely be avoided, especially if you suffer with depression, and some that are encouraged:

Foods to Avoid

Sugar

Sugar and sugary foods are absorbed quickly into the bloodstream, causing highs followed by lows when the sugars has passed through the body, leaving you feeling low in energy and tired. Imagine the emotional rollercoaster ride that your body goes on if you have sugar regularly.

Processed food

White flour products, such as white bread, cereal and pasta, does as much damage for your blood sugar levels as sugar itself.

Alcohol

Depression sufferers need to limit or avoid alcohol as it is a central nervous system depressant that has a direct effect on the brain. Essential vitamins are used to deactivate toxins in the liver, thereby depleting these nutrients that are essential for mental health and health in general.

Artificial sweeteners

Raw sugar, as bad as it is, is still better than artificial sweeteners, believe it or not. Neither are good for you but you have to choose the lesser of two evils, if you must choose at all! Artificial sweeteners block the production of the serotonin, causing mood dips and headaches, and can contribute to depression.

Foods to Eat

Omega-3 fats

These are your essential fats that contain a natural anti-depressant. They cannot be produced within your body so it is essential that they are taken in through your diet. Omega-3 fats can be found in oily fish such as salmon and sardines, as well as seeds and nuts, such as flaxseeds and almonds. Beef contains Omega-3 fats, as well as many vegetables such as Brussel sprouts, cauliflower, broccoli, spinach, kale and leeks. Surprisingly, strawberries, blackberries and raspberries also contact these essential fats. Too many people avoid fats for fear that they will become overweight, however, the right sort of fats like these Omega-3s actually help with maintaining a healthy weight.

Vitamin Bs

Vitamin B-1, Thiamin, has been associated with mood control and can be found in trout, pork, Macadamia nuts, sunflower seeds, oatmeal, peas, sweetcorn, brown rice, oranges eggs and asparagus. Vitamin B-9, or as it is more commonly known, folic acid, is necessary for mental and physical health. A significant number of studies suggest that there is a connection between a folic acid deficiency and depression. It is also suggested that a folic acid deficiency can reduce the effectiveness of anti-depressant drugs. Folic acid can be found in yeast extract, beans, legumes, citrus fruit, bananas, grain products and green leafy vegetables.

Vitamin B-12 is another B vitamin that has vital nutrients that help control depression and, again, can be found in foods such as fish, lean meat, chicken, eggs and milk.

High-fibre carbohydrates

Whole grains, brown rice, oatmeal, sweet potato, and whole wheat pasta contain high-fibre carbohydrates, which are naturally rich in an amino acid called tryptophan. Your body needs tryptophan, an essential amino acid, which is converted in our bodies into serotonin (the feel-good hormone).

Water

Not drinking enough water has a significant impact on mental health. Studies show a strong connection between depression and dehydration, as 85% of our brain is water. Dr Longmore, author of The Serotonin Secret, said: *"Not getting enough (water) can cause a chemical imbalance. People should drink at least one-and-a-half litres of water a day."*

Exercise

Exercise has significant benefits for our mental health. It can also help prevent people from becoming depressed in the first place. Exercise produces endorphins. Endorphins are endogenous opioid polypeptide compounds. They are produced by the pituitary gland and the hypothalamus in vertebrates during exercise, excitement, pain, consumption of spicy food and orgasm, and they resemble the opiates in their abilities to produce analgesia and a feeling of well-being. Endorphins also work as "natural pain relievers". The term "endorphin" implies a pharmacological activity, as opposed to a specific chemical formulation. It consists of two parts: endo- and -orphin; these are short forms of the words endogenous and morphine, intended to mean "a morphine-like substance originating from within the body".

In plain English, endorphins are our happy hormones and you can never have too many of these, especially if you are prone to depression. In some cases, it is possible to exercise your way out of mild to moderate depression. A simple brisk walk for 30 minutes every day can produce enough endorphins to keep you mentally and physically healthy.

Creativity

Winston Churchill, one of the greatest leaders of our time, suffered with recurrent episodes of depression. He was also highly creative and he used his writing to keep what he called his "black dog" at bay. Writing and other creative activities such as painting, gardening and music can offer a release that eases the mind and soul. The association between bipolar disorder and creativity first appeared in literature in the 1970s, but the idea of a link between "madness" and "genius" is much older, dating back at least to the time of Aristotle. Clearly, Winston Churchill was an exceptional man who led the United Kingdom during an intensely difficult wartime, but also penned more words than Shakespeare and Dickens put together.

Sufferers of depression can use creative outlets to express themselves or release whatever they have suppressed inside. I have found that creativity has provided me with a necessary distraction, which in itself lifted a great deal of weight from my weary mind. Modern lifestyle and work style don't help us either, as we limit our senses and experiences to mostly looking at a screen of some sort, so we lose our energy. Creativity energises and inspires. When did you last make something with your hands? You don't need to be depressed to be creative; we all need to use our hands and our hearts regularly. We all need to get out of our own head and escape to someplace else. It's good for us to let go and be creative. It is good for business, family life, and simply for personal satisfaction too.

Anti-depressants

For too many years, I resisted anti-depressants. To me, they were chemical and unnatural. I feared I'd become slow and lethargic as the drug took over my life. Guilt even prevented me from trying them as I thought people would look down on me. I struggled for more years than I needed to but learned a lot along the way. I managed and, to a certain degree, beat my depression through exercise, diet, positive thoughts and various other activities that I learned to do to take care of my mental health.

It was under control then one day it fell apart. I ran out of strength and energy to do what I needed to do not to be depressed. It all came crashing down and I let go! The story is too long and would fill another book if I described the build up to the breakdown but, in a nutshell, I was burned out and didn't see it coming. It was a different type of depression, which is why I didn't see the signs as I usually would. I had coped and coped and coped with one crisis after another, personal problems at home, and a brand new business. That night, I was due to speak at the Chamber of Commerce and was juggling children, picking up the babysitter and figuring out dinner, while practicing my little talk. By the time I reached my friend, who was babysitting for me, I had lost the plot. Looking back, she must have been shocked as I am certain that she had never seen me spew so much venom in my life. Usually, I was very positive and happy. She heard it all that evening as the tears rolled down my face. When she finally got a word in, she asked the dreaded question, "Angela, do you think that you are perhaps depressed?"

Her words hit my heart and I knew she was right. Why didn't I see it? How did I miss the signs? How did I get to this dark place and not even realise it? With mascara running down my face and a pile of snotty tissues, I announced to her that I was and that I was cancelling my Chamber event! Never in my life have I cancelled speaking, ever! I love speaking and I am the most reliable person I know. After letting it all out, I realised that I simply could not go on.

The story goes on but I will condense it for your benefit. After a conversation about anti-depressants with my kind friend, who was brave enough to state the obvious, and with my mother, I came to the decision that, if the doctor recommended anti-depressants, I would take them. He did and I did, and the results were life changing. For the first time in my life, I felt like I didn't have to do the work of not being depressed; the little white pills did the work for me. It felt as if I was having a holiday from depression and it was wonderful. I knew that they wouldn't "fix" me or solve the problem. It was still my responsibility to do all that I knew was right for my mental health, but having that nice, long break from the black cloud over my head was wonderful and I have absolutely no regrets. There are natural methods, there are things you can do to keep depression at bay, but I will never again stand in the way of anyone who would like to give anti-depressants a go. For me, it was exactly what I needed.

I Did It In My Pyjamas

Pyjama days are common, especially in winter. I no longer push myself each and every day because I know my limitations and I never want to get burned out again. Most of all, I want to enjoy every day of my life and I will not allow depression to rob me. If I have a bad night's sleep and don't have any early appointments, I try to go back to sleep for a couple more hours. Most mornings I am up at 5 or 6am, but there are mornings when I will sleep until 8am if I need to and not feel guilty for doing so.

A minimum of once a week, I have an introverted day in my pyjamas – sometimes twice a week, depending on the season (summer, I work outside as often as possible – sometimes in my pyjamas too!). It's just a little thing that I do that keeps me happy and takes the pressure off.

I have also learned a few ways of doing business in a way that works for me. When I am positive and perky (up), I make phone calls. When I am blue (down), I avoid the phone and take care of admin. There are days when I don't have a choice as my meetings are scheduled sometimes months in advance.

On those days, I have to get on with it, no matter how I feel. However, I have learned that if I have a busy day or two out of the office then I need to allow a day to work from home that week to balance things out. Knowing that the day at home is coming up helps me push myself when I have to be "out there". I can almost guarantee that anyone that I have done business with has no idea of this struggle and no idea that I am often chatting to them on the phone in my pyjamas! Does it matter? What matters is that I get the results that I want and enjoy the journey.

Do you push yourself too much to conform to what you perceive to be the acceptable way to run a business? Did you know that you can go for a run in the middle of the working day and call it business? Why not? It might be your best thinking time when you come up with a fantastic strategy to take your company forward. I have decided that from this year (it is January 2015 as I write), I am going to conduct as many meetings as possible by walking. I will ask if the person I am due to meet would prefer a coffee shop or a nice walk on the hill. Why do I have to sit down and drink coffee all the time? Clearly it is not good for my body, my physical and mental health. Training workshops are still being done the old-fashioned way at a boardroom table with our laptops. I haven't quite figured out how to get that one out of the box yet!

How Do You Do It?

This is how *I* did it with depression. I didn't make excuses but got on with living my dreams. You may or may not have depression but you may have excuses. What is holding you back right now? What can you do differently? Is there anything in your daily work routine that you can do differently to make the journey more enjoyable or more suitable to who you are? How do you stay inspired on down days? Do you have keys that you can use to stay happy and inspired? Do you have staff? Have you considered how they feel working for you? Do you allow them to work creatively, freely, and outside of the box, or do they have to sit in front of their computer all day long and punch out results? Do you ask their opinion? Do you get their feedback on how they would like to work?

I have asked you a few questions but there are many more to ask. Ask yourself questions until you find what works best for you, your family, and anyone that you do business with. You may be surprised and stumble across some great secrets that can change everything for the better. Perhaps you need a home day in your pyjamas, or perhaps you stay home too much and need to force yourself to get out there more. Only you know and only you can decide what is going to work best for you. The bottom line is that there are no rules. It is your life and you have the power to decide how to live it. If you are not happy then change things. If you are not happy, why not choose to be happy, no matter what curve ball life has thrown at you. If your staff are not happy, why not do something about it immediately? You can choose how you do it!

I Did it With Fear

"Feel the Fear and Do It Anyway."

- Susan Jeffers

Fear, failure or fun.

*S*leepless nights, lack of concentration, headaches, sore neck and shoulders, irritability, blotchy skin, flaky nails, nausea and so much more can stem from worry! How many business owners worry? I would guess that most business owners worry. They worry about bills, cash flow, staff, deadlines, quiet periods, busy periods, illness, lack of stock, failure and competition. I could go on and on but I am sure you can compile your own list of worries relevant to your business. Worry, however, is something you can control. You can choose not to worry. You can stop worrying. Or you can let worry get a hold of you and turn into a very real fear.

It's normal to have fear in life, you cannot avoid facing it, but it is what you do with it that counts. My first business fear started right at the beginning, the fear of starting a business. I feared just about everything from the obvious fear of failure, fear of charging real money, fear of not being good enough all the way to the fear of being a fraud. Cath Kidston so aptly said, *"When you are self-taught you always worry that you will be found out,"* and this is so true for many of us. We pick up and learn what we need along the way which makes us feel less of a business woman or man than those who have an MBA and other such letters after their names. Experiencing fear in business is a very real part of the journey. Some people fear starting a business so they never start at all whereas others fear starting but they push through that fear and get on with setting their business up. Every step of the way offers the option to back out due to fear or push through despite the fear.

"Every step of the way offers the option to back out due to fear or push through despite the fear."

Looking back I would say that my biggest fear to start off with was that I didn't really know anything worthwhile and was just a fraud. For the longest time I remember running workshops and doing talks appearing confident, but deep down inside I was terrified someone would catch me out and expose me. Mostly this stemmed from my lack of education since I never finished high school or had any formal training in anything. I would fear that someone would ask me a question that I could not answer, I would fear that they would stand up and shout out that I was talking nonsense and I would also fear that they would leave and talk behind my back about how rubbish my talk or training was. Now to be honest I think that the talking behind my back may have happened from time to time but not because my training was necessarily rubbish but simply because there are some people in this world that aren't happy unless they are gossiping or putting someone else down. I dealt with my fear of this quickly when I realised that it's their problem and not mine. If someone wants to learn they will learn from pretty much anything at all, even a "bad" talk or seminar. There is always something to learn!

Time was what healed me of some of my other fears. After some time had passed and I had trained quite a few women, I quickly realised that I honestly did have something to offer the world and that my self-taught experience has value. Fear also died down when I realised that it's OK not to have all the answers and so if someone asked a question that I couldn't answer, I would simply say that I didn't know but would find out for them.

Practice truly does make perfect but it also eliminates most of the fear. Every now and then I still get fearful about what people think of me when I stand up in front of them but I have trained myself to get my mind focused by telling myself the truths that I have chosen to believe such as:

- It doesn't matter what people think
- I don't have to know everything
- My experience qualifies me
- I am good at what I do
- Only speak about what I know that I know

I have been tempted many times to get my MBA, in fact I even applied to one university and got accepted based on my years of experience in running a business. It's incredible that I don't have a high school diploma but could have gone straight into an MBA program. Anyway, after much deliberation my very wise mother reminded me how much I didn't need a degree to do what I did and how much time and money it would take to get this something that I didn't need. I have since learned to value experience but at the same time continue to learn, study and read so that I am constantly growing in my area of expertise.

Strangely enough I never suffered from the common fear of being a woman and mother. It never crossed my mind that this would disqualify me in any way and although I know many women struggle with this I just didn't. I believed that if I could do a job well and served my superiors well I would advance. In my mind it had nothing to do with agenda but purely hard work, attitude and the desire to get ahead. I often wonder if the glass ceiling that so many women refer to isn't more a lack of confidence than men holding women back. In all my workplaces in all my life I don't ever recall being held back for being a woman. So this isn't a fear I personally can relate to but I know many to fear that invisible glass ceiling. You know, the quickest way to make it go away is to stop believing it exists and then just go for it and get to where you want to be. We live in a very modern age where there really are very few boundaries anymore.

Cash flow – or lack thereof – now that's something I have feared. My first company failed plain and simply because I ran out of money so borrowed and then borrowed some more to keep the company going until I had to admit defeat and close it down. So when I started the Women's Business Club I was frighteningly aware of the importance of a healthy bottom line with plenty of back up cash. I dealt with this fear by saving up as much as possible in a reserve account before I even considered taking any salary from the company. Once I reached a reserve that I thought would keep the company going for at least three months should anything go wrong, I feared less. Despite this theory there have been a few difficult months when large, unexpected expenses have cropped up wiping out our reserves – which resulted in some fear, I can assure you. So how do I "feel the fear and do it anyway" in these situations you might ask? Quite simply, I keep going even when quitting would have been acceptable. I made the decision that it's not over until it's over so kept pushing forward through hard times and it has paid off.

So what is fear then? Simply put, fear is your brain's reaction to a stressful stimulus. This reaction then causes a chemical reaction that causes several physical reactions in your body such as a raised heart rate, shallow breathing and sweaty palms, collectively known as the fight-or-flight response. The fear reaction that kick starts the subsequent reactions is involuntary. We don't choose to fear, fear is an automatic reaction. Without fear we would not survive, it is an essential instinct to a perceived threat. Experiencing fear from time to time is a normal part of life.

The difference between worry and fear is that you have greater control over worry than you do over fears. Fear happens before you know it! The first way to get rid of unnecessary fear in your life is to start with addressing your worries. Take stock of what you worry about and see what you can do to eliminate them either by finding a solution or by training yourself to have a positive mindset. The bottom line is that worry is a useless emotion that cannot ever achieve anything in your life or your business. Ditch worry!

Once you have addressed worries you can see what fears are left. So fear is a normal part of life and is essential for our survival. If we don't have any fear we will make unwise decisions or put ourselves into dangerous situations. However, some fear is unnecessary and should be overcome. Fear such as that related to public speaking, failure, death, spiders and taking certain risks in business are very common. In many cases it is these very fears that stop people from moving forward and can seriously hinder business growth. You have to ask yourself a very important question. The question very simply is, "So *what* if it's scary?" Tell yourself that you *can* do it! If I can do it anyone can. Fear is an unpleasant emotion caused by the threat of danger, pain, or harm. The key word there is that fear is an *emotion*. Fear (and worry) comes from your mind, from your thoughts. You have a thought which triggers an emotion which could be fear. Your heart begins to pound and even if you realise that there is nothing to be fearful of, your body remains in a fearful state until something is done to calm you down.

There are various degrees of fear from a fright or startle to crippling fear. Fear comes in many forms such as nervousness, terror, panic or anxiety. Stage fright is a form of fear. Anxiety is a fear of a future event or something out of your control. Shock is an instantly gripping fear and horror is an intense disgust or revulsion sort of fear. Hysteria can result from fear and so can a heart attack along with very many other side effects or consequences stemming from this emotion.

Fear can be expressed in various ways ranging from a scream to paralysis to diarrhoea. In order to avoid dire consequences, you will need to learn to express fear in a healthy way rather than allow fear to control your mind and your body. Especially in business!

Fear in Business

Let's take a look at some of the common fears that we face in business and what we can do to deal with them wisely:

Cash Flow

No cash equals no business, so a common fear is a lack of cash flow. Many business owners, especially women in business, fear charging what they are worth which has an obvious effect on cash flow too. Some business owners don't take care of the bottom line and borrow more than they can afford to pay back, ultimately damaging the business. So what is the best way to deal with cash flow fears? Here are some basics that all businesses can put in place to ensure peace of mind in the area of cash flow:

- Maintain a cash flow forecast.
- Keep expenses lower than income at all times.
- Build up a reserve account from 20% of your income.
- Where possible take up front payment.
- Invoice quickly with clear payment terms.

"He who fears he will suffer, already suffers from his fear."

- Michel de Montaigne

Time

Running out of time is a common fear for small business owners as they are at that stage where they have to do everything from make the tea, clean the toilet and do the filing to making sales and negotiating with clients. Here are some basics that all businesses can put in place to ensure peace of mind in the area of time:

- Outsource tasks that someone can do better than you.
- Reduce time spent in meetings and travelling.
- Set a clear timeframe for marketing and social media.
- Schedule breaks in your day.
- Ditch multitasking and focus on one task at a time.
- Create a system for your paperwork and electronic files.

Growth

Strangely enough, a common fear can be growth. Too many businesses get stuck into a comfortable rut and the thought of taking the necessary steps to grow scares them nearly to death. They fear business taking over their whole life, they fear the risk that is involved with growth and they could even fear not knowing what to do with the growth. Some businesses fail where they should have grown. Here are some basics that all businesses can put in place to ensure peace of mind in the area of growth:

- Systemise your business and manage the system.
- Find the right people to work within your system.
- Create boundaries to protect and enjoy your personal life.
- Surround yourself with wise business owners.
- Believe that you are capable of growth.
- Don't take risks with consequences that you aren't willing to bear if you fail.

Competition

Most business owners fear their competition. They run their business with one eye on their competitors at all times. Although it's good to check on your competitors from time to time I prefer to run my lane with blinkers on most of the time. That way I can focus on the goal or the finish line and get on with my race. People will always copy the best, the one who is ahead. My philosophy is that as long as I stay ahead then I will always be the original and they will be the copy. Here are some basics that all businesses can put in place to ensure peace of mind in the area of competition:

- Build a relationship with your customers.
- Meet their need or solve their problems.
- Don't drop your prices to compete.
- Stay ahead and stay fresh.
- Continually connect with new people.
- Innovate, create and set the trends.

Reputation

You can't please all of the people all of the time. There will be times when people just won't like you. Even worse, there will be times when people won't like you and will have no problems spreading the word about their dislikes. Press releases may pop up with nasty things about you, blog posts and perhaps even car bumper stickers. Who knows, but living in fear of damaging your reputation will severely limit your potential. Here are some basics that all businesses can put in place to ensure peace of mind in the area of reputation:

- Always be honest.
- Accept that some people won't like you, ever.
- Treat all people with respect and kindness.

Public Speaking

Public speaking is the number one fear for many people. It's right up there with fear of death, snakes and spiders! But for a small business owner, being able to communicate well to a group is crucial. Communication can simply be a sixty second elevator pitch at an event or it can involve giving a talk to a group of people. No matter what form of public you speak to, work on being the best you can be and you will make the right impression. Here are some basics that all businesses can put in place to ensure peace of mind in the area of public speaking:

- Practice, practice, practice.
- Take slow deep breaths before speaking.
- Visualise yourself as a successful speaker.

Be Prepared

Preparing well in any given situation will usually get rid of unnecessary fears. Many times when I do a talk I am unable to think so whatever I have prepared just comes out of my mouth. If I haven't prepared well I would end up saying "um" a lot! If you are fearful of writing an exam the most obvious thing to do is to study. Being prepared deals with a good portion of the fear. The same applies in business, don't wing it, be prepared for as much as possible. If you are going to see a client then why not make sure you read up about them first on LinkedIn and their website. If you are going to do a presentation be prepared by having a backup of your notes or electronic devices if it's essential that you use them. Charge your device batteries and carry a charger with you. Think of everything that could go wrong and if it will be detrimental to the meeting plan a backup – that way, when you get there you will have less fear and will be more able to concentrate on the things you need to.

If your business involves flowers or food, prepare beforehand by practicing and tasting. Flowers can be damaged by hotels' heating systems, so if you are doing a display and have to leave it overnight then ensure that you have a backup of any delicate flowers. There are so many examples for all sorts of situations but the bottom line is that being prepared can only be good for you and should reduce any fears you may have.

Fear Control Tips

Fear and anxiety can feel as if they control us leaving us feeling like there is nothing we can do about a situation, but we have much more control than we realize. AWARE is an acronym that can help us deal with worry and fear. It stands for:

A: Accept
W: Watch
A: Act
R: Repeat
E: Expect

A: Accept the anxiety. Don't try to fight it. Decide just to go with the experience. Fighting your anxiety, allowing anger to rise up or being scared just fuels the fire.

W: Watch the anxiety. Just watch it, by imagining that you are able to step out of yourself and watch yourself. As you watch, control your breathing by taking deep in-breaths followed by longer out-breaths. Observe yourself and the fear without judging it to be good or bad.

A: Act normally. Carry on talking or behaving as if nothing is different. This sends a powerful signal to your unconscious mind that its over-dramatic response is actually not needed because nothing unusual is going on. If you run from the situation, your immediate anxiety will of course decrease but this won't help you deal with future fear. Staying in the situation helps you learn to control your panic response and trains your mind to deal with fear objectively. This is why people often say that the first few minutes of any activity that you fear are the worst. My heart always races before going on a stage to sing or speak but once I get into it the fear stops and I always end up enjoying myself.

R: Repeat. Repeat the above steps in your mind if necessary. Practice makes perfect. The more you condition yourself with the steps above the more you will be able to control your fear responses. Each time you take control of your fear will give you a deeper conviction that you do not need to let fear be in control.

E: Expect the best. One of the greatest feelings in life is the realisation that you can control fear much more than you thought possible. What you fear may never happen and allowing yourself to fear things can take up a huge portion of your emotional energy which could be better spent in other areas.

Eliminating Fear

The exercise above helps us to control fear once it has hit us, after our heart has started to race. However, I have long searched for a way to avoid fear completely. As I mentioned previously, before going on stage I would struggle with stage fright. Not only would I experience a racing heart and breathlessness but I would also have to run to the loo as diarrhoea hit me each and every time. I was not a pretty sight before going on stage and worst of all, I would suffer with breathlessness while on stage, which again is not ideal when singing or speaking. This struggle led me to search for a remedy and I came up with my own ABC:

A: Attitude

One of the first things that I discovered was that my attitude toward what I was doing had a huge effect on my delivery. My emphasis was too much on myself, on what people would think about me, on how they would receive what I was saying. When singing, I feared that they would judge the fact that I cannot sing very well, etc. My entire attitude was quite a selfish one. I learned to shift the focus onto them. I did this by reminding myself that I am on the stage to serve them. It's not about me but about them.

I learned to acknowledge that it didn't really matter what they thought of me. After all, there would always be those that loved what I presented and those that would not. I accepted that I could not, and never would, be able to please everyone in my audience and in fact it wasn't my place to do so. My place was to deliver what I was asked to deliver to the best of my ability and leave what I have delivered with the audience. This change in attitude significantly took the pressure off.

I also changed my attitude toward things such as perfectionism, learning that no speaker ever delivered a perfect message and no singer ever sung perfectly. The aim isn't perfection but engagement and so I learned to engage with the audience rather than try to be perfect in my delivery. This too took the pressure off as the audience and I both enjoyed ourselves far more when I was authentic.

B: Breathing

As with all things to do with emotions, I used breathing control methods to stay calm and I kept myself hydrated by drinking plenty of water beforehand. Usually I try to drink quite a lot of water from about two hours before I have to be on stage but then stop drinking about half an hour before so that I am not left on the stage with a full bladder, which could turn out to be quite awkward! Simple breathing techniques such as the ones mentioned previously do the job well, deep breaths in and longer breaths out.

Most importantly, when you are doing your breathing exercises keep your thinking in check too so that you don't counteract the effect of the breathing with nervous thoughts.

C: Confidence

Taking time to concentrate on what is true rather than all the colourful things that your mind can throw at you is essential to eliminating fear. Firstly, I would concentrate on my message or song so that I could really absorb it into my being. Concentrating on things such as, "What will they think?" or "I don't think this message is good enough," or "I can't sing." Will all deliver the wrong message to your body and ultimately could even be a self-fulfilling prophecy. Confidence is a choice. You decide to be confident. You decide that what you have to offer is valuable. No one else can make these internal decisions for you.

Confidence can be gained and confidence can be lost. *So do not throw away your confidence; it will be richly rewarded.* Understanding this valuable principle has helped me get through so many of life's situations really well. The first time I realised that confidence was my choice and something that I could project was in a job interview. It occurred to me that I can choose what I say and how I say it, so I chose to say some well-rehearsed lines while remaining as authentic as I could. After discovering this little secret, I pretty much got every job I wanted. Prior to this revelation, I was riddled with fear in interviews and had to endure many interviews before receiving a job offer. After gaining confidence I lost all fear in the interview process, carefully selected the jobs that *I* wanted and then proceeded to accept interviews when I was sure that the job was exactly what I wanted. I saved a great deal of time and vast amounts of negative emotional energy simply by being confident.

This little nugget has kept me going through all sorts of situations that I would once have responded to with fear. However, when I first started trying out confidence, I did have bouts of arrogance. Arrogance is the evil twin sister of confidence, it's ugly and will get you nowhere. Don't confuse the two just because they look similar and dress in the same clothes. Arrogance will get you nowhere fast, confidence will get you ahead quickly. Confidence is self-assurance, poise and self-belief whereas arrogance is self-importance, conceit and pride. *Do not think of yourself more highly than you ought to think, but think soberly[i].* People generally resist arrogant people whereas confident people are irresistible. Being a humble person does not mean that you lack confidence. Quiet confidence is very attractive as opposed to loud, prideful arrogance which really turns people off.

Living life without fear or with minimal fear is a wonderful way to live. Eliminating fear means that we can free up emotional space to enjoy some of the other emotions.

"You have to accept whatever comes, and the only important thing is that you meet it with the best you have to give."

- Eleanor Roosevelt

Fear of the competition is a common fear too but the way I see it is that there is plenty of business to go around. From time to time I do a competitor analysis just because I am curious, but most of the time I simply run in my own lane and look ahead to what I perceive to be the prize – no matter what my competitors are doing. I am confident that what we offer at Women's Business Club meets a need and as long as we are meeting a need we have nothing to fear. The day we stop offering solutions to problems and start to try and sell our services no matter what, we will fall. Fear causes businesses to charge too little, offer too many discounts and generally undervalue what they do.

The stone in your shoe

When we fear we stop taking action, we become passive. Long term passivity can lead to stagnation and we all know how unappealing stagnant water can be, even more so a stagnant business. Seeing the sorry state of our business because of the lack of action causes us to lose confidence resulting in even less action. Fear can easily cause a downward spiral into a sea of negativity. Experiencing fear in business is normal but it is what we do with it that counts. Do not allow fear near the "remote control" of your business.

Do not allow fear to hit pause or even stop. Do not allow fear to rob you of your confidence. Yes, you will feel fear from time to time but it doesn't need to stop you from moving forward. Make a decision that you will feel the fear and do it anyway, that way fear will have little hold over you. It will be like a stone in your shoe that you simply remove so you can carry on walking. It's a simple analogy but it does the trick. You feel a stone in your shoe, it is uncomfortable, possibly painful. The logical solution is to stop walking, find the stone, remove it and then keep walking. This solution means that the stone was a minor setback but it didn't throw you off course.

The other option is for you to try and ignore that there is a stone in your shoe and continue walking. After a few steps you experience some pain as the stone cuts into your foot. Sometime later you end up with a bloody wound in your foot as the stone rubs away your flesh. Still, you try to pretend it is not there and continue walking. Eventually your foot gets infected and you end up completely off course as you change direction and head for the doctor's surgery. And all because you wouldn't stop and face the silly little stone in your shoe.

At the first sign of fear, make a conscious decision to deal with it and not to ignore it. For example, when I realised I feared public speaking I actually decided to deal with it by doing lots of public speaking. At first I felt really nauseous and short of breath beforehand and very depressed afterwards. In time it became a lot easier. I cannot imagine where I would be today if I ignored my fear of public speaking. To think of all the opportunities I would have missed out on and all the wonderful people I have met as a result. That little stone didn't get the best of me.

The best part is that where there was once no confidence there is now a great deal of confidence. Lack of confidence and fear go hand in hand, so dealing with one automatically deals with the other. As your confidence goes your fear grows! On the flip side, as your confidence grows you fear goes. Working on your confidence will automatically work on your fear.

Familiarity breeds contempt

Fear often keeps us in our comfort zones. We like what we know. We feel safe with the familiar. Why fix what isn't broken, right? Wrong! Well in some cases wrong, let's be honest, sometimes it is great to leave something well alone if it is working well. The key is to know the difference between what should be changes and what should be left ticking over. But I guess that is a whole other subject, so let's get back to familiarity.

In business, just like in a relationship, we can get familiar and start to take things and people for granted. Sticking with the relationship analogy, we work really hard at first when we are dating holding nothing back to win the person that our heart is set on. After some time though, it all gets a bit tiring so we slack off a bit. The relationship seems fine so we slack off a little more. Slowly but surely we stop taking risks and get comfortable and familiar with what we have. Of course, anyone who has ever been in a relationship will tell you that it doesn't work that way. You have to keep things fresh and exciting at times. Familiarity causes arguments and ultimately the breakdown of a relationship. Business is no different. At first you are passionate and work your butt off but after time things start to tick over nicely so you sit back and relax a bit. Business continues to tick over so you get comfortable. Sadly, while you are resting on your laurels feeling pleased with what you have built, your competitors are innovating and keeping fresh. They have chosen not to get comfortable and avoid the fear, but they are facing the fear head on and using it to propel themselves forward. Just like a good relationship, they have chosen to keep the spark alive, take risks and keep trying new things.

Their staff is fresh and excited, their clients are enthused and the general public are aware of their existence even if they don't use their products or services just yet. Risk involves an element of fear but it is the risk that stops the business (or relationship) from get stale and boring. Take a chance every now and then, try new things, think outside the box and see how your business will grow from strength to strength. A little bit of fear to get the adrenalin pumping can be a good thing. It's up to you to monitor how much you would like to play with.

"No amount of security is worth the suffering of a life lived chained to a routine that has killed your dreams."

- Kent Nerburn

Fear of the unknown

Indian born Lord Karan Bilimoria launched Cobra Beer in the midst of a recession. In 1989, along with his friend Arjun Reddy, Karan founded Cobra Beer in a little flat in Fulham. The idea for the beer had come up while he was a student at Cambridge, where he regularly ate his meals at Indian restaurants. He noticed that regular lager was too gassy and bloating to be enjoyed with food, while ale was too bitter to accompany a meal. He came up with a concept for a beer that had "the refreshing qualities of a lager" but the "smoothness and drinkability of an ale" to accompany food – in particular, Indian food and curry.

At the time Karan had a student debt of £20,000 and funds to start the business were not easy to find. Borrowing money from various sources and £30,000 from a bank, Cobra commenced operations and Karan himself began distributing 15 cases of beer at a time across London in a battered old Citroen 2CV.

By 2007 Cobra was being sold in over 45 countries, and had a total production capacity of 450,000 cases per month. Revenues stood at £30 million and, with rapid expansion, were expected to cross £100 million by 2010. Just think of how fear of the unknown could have changed this story had Karan been crippled by it.

It seems ridiculous if you think about it but most of the time what we fear most is the unknown. Too often we hold ourselves back because we fear what we don't know. It's the same as saying that we don't know what we fear but we fear "it" anyway. What's the worst that can happen? I mentioned this key before but let's look at it again. In any situation where we do not know or have any control over the outcome, ask that very important question, "What's the worst that can happen?"

Let's look at a very common example, a financial decision. You have to take a chance and spend a large sum of money in your business. You feel a great deal of fear because you could make a mistake and lose it all. So ask yourself, "What's the worst that can happen?" The chances are that you only lose a bit of money but you have more or can make more. So really it's not worth wasting energy on fear is it? Perhaps it's not that simple, perhaps the sum you are risking could cost you your business. Once again, ask yourself, "What's the worst that can happen?" If you lose your business what would you do? Would you start all over again, would you get a job, would you retire or would you do something completely different? Whatever you answer, consider if it really is as bad as it seems. You could do this over and over again until you realise that whatever the risk and the outcome is, it's not as bad as it seems. Nothing is ever really as bad as it seems so we don't need to fear nearly as much as we do.

Now is as good a time as any to start your business.

I Did it by Redefining Success

"The moment one gives close attention to anything, even a blade of grass, it becomes a mysterious, awesome, indescribably magnificent world in itself."

- Henry Miller

What defines success, really?

uccess, failure, health, wealth, happiness and just about every-thing else starts in the mind. If we truly understood the power of our mind many lives would be significantly altered forever.

Our Beliefs Determine the Outcome

One of the biggest problems today is our perception and definition of success. One dictionary defines success *as the accomplishment of an aim or purpose* and another one defines it as *the attainment of wealth, position, hon-ours, or the like.* The meanings of these two definitions are worlds apart in many ways so it is vital that we create our own definition of success.

I listened to one of my club members recently who shared her observation after one of our Connect Business Lunches. As our guest speaker drove away in a shiny white Mercedes in her well pressed business suit she turned to me and said, "Now *she* is the real deal." As we walked she continued to share her perception with me saying, *"You can see that she knows what she is talking about as her life proves it."*

These brief comments got me thinking about success and the perception of success. I had struggled for quite some time about this in my own life. Since being in business I have remained in the same house and have driven the same car. My plan is to upgrade only when it becomes necessary but I grew more and more concerned about the impression I was giving those whom I was leading in the business world. People, especially women, are extremely judgemental of each other and I am aware that I need to give the right impression within 30 seconds when meeting someone new. Being an introvert, I really struggle with this and have to work extra hard at being friendly and welcoming within these few seconds. Introverts are known to take time to warm to people and can often seem aloof when they are in fact merely introverted. This is a fact I have been aware of and work hard at combating as I believe a friendly welcome is one of the most important parts of our club.

But let's get back to the comments about the "real deal" woman. I gave these comments some thought and concluded that none of us knew her well enough to know if she had in fact bought the Mercedes herself or if her husband or parents had bought it for her. Alternatively, had she worked very hard at her successful image at the expense of her financial freedom only to find herself desperately drowning in debt? Or, had she lost a loved one and inherited a large sum of money? We don't know and can only play a guessing game. She may well have been successful at her business and bought her car and nice clothes entirely on her own merit without any debt whatsoever. Again, we simply don't know. But it was the appearance of "success" that had a few women in awe which led them to believe that she was the "real deal".

"My success is how I feel about my journey and accomplishments not how you feel about them. And in this place I find complete freedom because I don't need to impress anyone or bother with what they think."

How do people perceive you? Do you look the part? Are you appearing successful by everyone else's standards when you are out there? Do I look the part to you? How do you judge me when you see me? Do you judge my humble home and little Lexus as successful or not successful? Would you change your opinion if I told that you that I intend to remain in my humble home until I have saved up enough money to buy my dream farm cash? Would you be impressed then? How would you perceive me if I drove a different car or had a chauffeur driven limousine? No matter how you perceive me I know that I am successful. This is the most important thing to me. My success is how I feel about my journey and accomplishments, not how others feel about them. And in this place I find complete freedom because I don't need to impress anyone or bother with what they think.

Write Your Own Definition of Success

Don't rely on the dictionary or other people in your world to write your definition of success for you. You have one life and it's up to you to create it every step of the way. At the end of your life you cannot blame anyone for the things you didn't do. Success is what you decide it to be so that you are content with the life you have built. What do *you* want? Why do you want it? What will make you completely content? What is important to you? Ask yourself these questions, they are extremely important. If you don't know the answers dig deep until you figure them out.

"There is only one success – to be able to spend your life in your own way."

- Christopher Morley

How do you want to spend your days? What is your dream? What is important to *you*? More questions that need answers. But before we start digging let's take a look at some very important things that could be affecting your definition and perception of success.

Stop Judging Others and Judge Yourself

Did you ever hear that little saying when you were a child at school, "When you point one finger, there are three fingers pointing back to you"? Well it really is true. Judging others is hard work and only highlights your own flaws. Do you remember the other saying we used to taunt at school, "It takes one to know one"? This classic retort to an insult dates from the early 1900s and is also absolutely true. We only pickup on the flaws of others that already exist in us or we become insecure around those who have clearly excelled in an area we know we fail in.

There have been two occasions in my life when I was faced with these harsh truths. My husband has been the iron that sharpens my iron – we sharpen each other. Ashamedly I confess to you that I used to resort to name calling in an argument until for some reason one day every word that I said seemed to hit me in the face. I realised that I was not only insulting and hurting him but I was also describing myself in doing so. I quickly learned after that eye-opening day to think before I lashed out at him, to consider if what I was saying would come right back to me. Every single time it did. Whatever I intended to say to him was actually describing me to a tee. I quickly learned to examine myself based on what I wanted to say to him and I am happy to report that I no longer resort to childish name calling but also that we seldom argue now too.

The second occasion was when a good friend said something very innocent to me and my daughter. She said, "You two are very alike which explains why you clash." It wasn't those words as much as our reaction to them which opened my eyes. We both instantly took a step away from each other and in chorus said, "NO WE ARE NOT!" Needless to say the truth hurt both of us as we didn't get along very well. My teenage daughter didn't have the maturity to learn from that very revealing moment but I did my best to use it to my advantage for my personal growth. From that day my senses have been heightened around her, whenever she annoys me with something she says or does, I try to contain myself and quickly check whether or not I have the same character flaws. Nine times out of ten I do. It has been a very humbling exercise and I have used it to help me chip away some nasty edges from my character.

In both cases it was far more beneficial for me to judge myself than to judge others. Family and friends, people who know us well and whom we see on a regular basis, offer fantastic opportunities for self-examination and growth. If you are brave enough you could even ask them for feedback from time to time on what you are doing well and what needs improvement. Getting into the habit of doing this rather than judging others will soften you towards people and make you more compassionate. You will quickly realise that everyone is struggling through life in one way or another. No one has it all figured out and we need to be kind to each other on this journey called life.

Stop Comparing Yourself to Others

Stop comparing yourself to others; compare yourself with who you were and what you accomplished a year ago.   Men and women all over the world are trying to be like someone else. Very few have figured out that you are better off being an original than a copy of someone else. Be yourself not someone else. Take time, years if that's what it takes, to discover who you are. Finding yourself and loving yourself is one of the most powerful things that you could ever do. Success will follow automatically.

"Today you are You, that is truer than true. There is no one alive who is Youer than You."

- Dr. Seuss

Life can feel like a tiring and endless race and success just a word that will never become a reality for you. Do you feel like you are daily jumping onto a treadmill that is set too fast and you can't keep up or does it feel more like you are running in a hamster wheel and no matter how hard you try you simply cannot get anywhere? It's quite easy to see why it's called the rat race isn't it?

Let's make success less of an abstract and help you define it in a way that it is personal and attainable. Once you have stopped judging others and comparing yourself to others, you are ready to begin. Our next step is to kill some sacred cows.

Sacred cow number 1: Success is a destination.

You may often hear yourself say things like, "When I achieve this or when that happens then I will be successful". A financial value could be assigned to success or a physical location. For example, "When I have made my first million I will be a success" or "When we have made it in Paris we have succeeded". Absolutely anything that starts with a "when" in order to describe what you think will determine your success is a myth, an illusion. You will never feel successful if your definition of success starts with a "when".

Success is a journey and the sooner you get on the right path the sooner you will live a successful life that is fulfilling and offers contentment. No number or destination can offer success or fulfilment; something will always be missing leaving you to chase after another "when". "What" and "How" are, however, reasonable questions to ask. "What is success?" and "How can I achieve it?" will get you to a place where you will feel successful. It won't be a specific destination but it might be a specific achievement. Contentment is a choice and so is happiness. Once you can master the ability to be content despite the circumstance and to be happy within yourself rather have that than based on how other people make you feel, then you are on the right path to success no matter how you define it.

Truth number 1: Success is a journey.

A great way to enjoy a journey is to have both a journey planner and a travel diary. The planner helps you find your way from where you are to where you want to be. In the Women's Business Club we have several very practical planning tools that help our business women create a map for the journey that they desire to take. We have developed the revolutionary Achieve Success Map as well as our fantastic Vision Map. These tools help women take control of their future and map it out as best they can according to what they perceive success to be. Some women want to plan more family time, some want to make more money and others want to expand their business to an international level. The journey planner is a great way to decide where you want to be and plan a way to get there.

The travel diary, or as we call it, the success diary, is a great tool for recording and remembering where you have come from. You record the ups and downs, good days and bad days. Add ticket stubs, photographs and dried flowers – whatever you like to remind you of your business journey. Nearly all business owners say that nothing seems to happen fast enough. However, if you record your journey and reflect back on it from time to time you will end up being greatly encouraged by how much you do actually achieve.

Sacred cow number 2: Success is the absence of failure.

Failure is essential to success. I firmly believe that you cannot achieve success without failure. Playing life safe to avoid failure will also mean that you avoid living. Failure means breakdown, letdown, collapse and disappointment according to the dictionary but what the dictionary fails to do is to capture the greater meaning of the word. Yes, failure can be a great letdown and disappointment but you can redefine the word to suit you.

"I honestly think it is better to be a failure at something you love than to be a success at something you hate."

- George Burns

Failure can mean lessons learned, opportunity, direction and discovery. How you interpret this one powerful word is entirely your choice and that choice will determine who you will go on to become. Can failure define you? Yes. Can failure hold you back? Yes. Can failure make you a success? Yes. Can failure be a useful tool in your life? Yes. Failure is exactly whatever you allow it to be. Failure is **just a word** to describe an experience – often an isolated experience. What you *do* with that word and that experience is what will make or break you and possibly affect you for the rest of your life. The power of failure lies in your *perception* of the word!

"The power of failure lies in your perception of the word!"

Truth number 2: Success comes from failure.

As soon as you start to believe that failure is the stepping stone to success then you will begin to fail (and succeed) with gusto. If the only way to the top was to step on failure, wouldn't you just take the necessary steps? Of course you would! So get busy with trying, failing and trying again. The end result will be success – all you have to do is fail enough times to get there.

Jumping to the *doing it in the bath* theme, is taking long baths during the working day a recipe for failure or success? It all depends how you look at it, what you achieve in the bath and what your view of success and failure is. I choose to give myself thinking time when I need it or feel overwhelmed.

I think in the bath, in the garden or go for long walks and sometimes even have a nap. A random connection? Perhaps, but what I am trying to show you is how our perceptions of things might be the very thing that is hindering us from experiencing the freedom that we need on our journey to success.

Sacred cow number 3: Success is having it all.

No one has it all, no one ever. There is no such thing as having it all. Everyone has something missing in their life. When we look up to those who we perceive to have it all it is our perception not their reality. What does having it all mean to you right now? Do you have a list of what you want? Will fulfilment of that list mean that you have succeeded? What if one of the things on your list gets taken off for some reason after you have acquired it, do you go from success to failure? And, when you have achieved what is on your list that makes you successful, then what? A new list? Retirement? What happens next when you achieve success? Have you ever met anyone who has it all? Perhaps ask them if they feel peaceful and fulfilled or are they still striving for more? I think you would find it a very interesting exercise and I am certain you will be shocked with what you find.

Truth number 3: Success is having enough.

Success is being satisfied with what you have right now no matter what that might mean. This doesn't mean that you will not advance or work hard to get to the next level from where you are at. What it does mean is that you are not stressing and striving. It means that you have decided to be grateful for what you have and to find peace and satisfaction in your current circumstances. That way, a change in circumstance won't devastate you. If what you have right now isn't enough then you will never have enough. You will always need more.

Sacred cow number 4: Success is getting ahead of others.

Some people feel that they will only be successful when they have achieved more than their competition. They keep their eyes on others around them and work very hard at staying ahead no matter what the cost. If someone should attempt to rise up against them in any way they will do their utmost to suppress them or put them down. People who will stop at nothing to have the success they desire are often ruthless, arrogant and selfish. It's not that they necessary decide to be that way but it is what their hunger for success makes them. Even the nicest person who focuses solely on their success can turn nasty.

Truth number 4: Success is empowering others.

The key to attaining and maintaining true success is actually by serving and empowering others. It is when you bring out the best in others that you automatically rise to the top. Empowering your team could even mean telling them not to work, to take some time off, to go shopping or have a bath! It can also mean rewarding failures as well as successes and it can mean making them look good, even in front of the people that *you* actually want to impress. You cannot lose by empowering others, what goes around always comes back around.

Sacred cow number 5: Success will make you popular.

Success can create a bitter taste in your mouth, because instead of being happy about your achievements, people can be mean to you. Success stirs up jealousy, bitterness and resentment. Insecure people will try and bring you down and put you in your place. Your success could highlight their lack of success, making them miserable. It would be easy to become bitter when people start to dislike you when you have done well in business or in any area of life. However, what I do is I feel pity for them as it shows that they still have a lot to learn. When possible, I do my best to encourage the people that are mean to me but more often than not they prefer to cut me off entirely which

100

is always sad. The best thing we can do is to ensure that we wear any measure of success well without any pride or arrogance. It's also important to block your ears to a lot of what is said. Absorbing every comment, either good or bad, can have a significant impact on you, it's best simply not to listen.

Truth number 5: Success is a great responsibility.

As Spider Man so aptly said, "With great power comes great responsibility." Yes there is a level of power with success as success attracts people and gives you a platform for influence. You cannot control who hears and reads about you but you can choose what you do with any influence you have gained. If you recognise that you have a responsibility and act accordingly you will do well. It's not about popularity but about influence and what you choose to do with it.

But then that all depends on what your definition of success is. I turned to Facebook and asked the Women's Business Club followers what success meant to them. The response was vast and varied:

"Success is achieving your original goals, and being able to adapt them to suit your business for continued growth and success."

- **Helen Tweddle**

"Success is continuing over and through hurdles, rather than stopping to cry at them or turn around to look back."

- **Fiona Jones**

"Success is being happy with what you do, making your customers happy too and at the same time making a living."

- **Elaine Mary Botfield**

"Success is when the vision you have becomes reality and turns into a viable business."

- **Karin Whittaker**

101

"Success is being able to enjoy the journey knowing that you are doing the best that you can and having fun doing it."

- **Rosalind Pattyn** (aka my mom)

"When your goods sell themselves without Facebook"

- **Dawn Ryder**

My husband's definition of success is fantastic; his definition of success is, "Getting up every day knowing that you are doing what you are meant to do with your life."

I hope that by now you are able to write down your own definition of success. My personal definition of success is:

- Being authentic (me).
- Maintaining my physical and mental health (my body).
- Doing what comes naturally from within and generating a financial profit from what I do (my work).
- Loving my God, my husband, my children and those closest to me (my world).
- Enjoying all of the above.

I consider myself successful when all of the above are working together in harmony. I feel less successful when I let one or more of the above slip. My faith and my family are very important to me, when I allow my work to negatively impact my family life then I am not successful. Enjoying life is vital in my opinion so when I do all of the above but don't enjoy it I know I am no longer successful. When all that I do comes from a place of me being me then I know I am successful. The second that I attempt to be someone I am not then everything else seems to fall apart and I know that I am no longer successful.

Personally, the above definition of success is a life long journey and I get better at it all the time. Right now I consider myself successful by my own definition. I wake up most mornings really excited about the day because I love my life and I love everything that I get to do in each day. Some days are more difficult but I accept that those are just "off" days and that the next day will be better.

The great thing about my definition of success is that it doesn't depend on any circumstance or material state. When I lived in poverty in South Africa I was as content as I am living in one of the wealthiest nations in the world with no personal financial worries. My success cannot be taken away from me and no matter what life throws at me, I can always be content and successful.

To me success is being able to take a bath in the middle of the day, read a book and call it working!

I Did it in the Bath

"If you love life and live it to the fullest there are limitless ways to spend your time."

- Richard Branson

Slowing down and smelling roses.

*T*his book was born in the bath. In fact most of my problems are solved in the bath and some of my greatest ideas come to me in the bath. Yes, I really enjoy a nice long hot bath and I have been known to take these lovely long hot baths in the middle of a working day too.

"What?" you gasp!

Who says a bath can't be a part of your business creative process? I seem to spend more time telling my team to stop working than I do telling them to work. Natalie, our South Wales Regional Director, was often surprised when I told her to take a day off, visit a friend or just play with her children. She was even more surprised when I told her that it will help her grow her business and make more money!

Dolce Far Niente

You see, one of the biggest problems with the way we view work today is our perception that success is and can only come as a result of physically working all the hours God sends. This simply isn't true. After watching *Eat, Pray, Love* I fell in love with the expression *dolce far niente,* which is an old Italian expression literally meaning "sweet doing nothing" or "the sweetness of doing nothing". It inspired me so I researched the phrase and internalised the concept. The thought of doing nothing made me cringe at first. It looked good in a movie but in reality, in my reality, it looked like a time waster. We can learn so much from our children, they don't sit and evaluate how they can squeeze as much as possible out of every minute but they simply live each day. I am determined to do the same. Facebook, Twitter, emails and other online activities can be the biggest thief of *dolce far niente* because they cause us to fill our sweet nothing moments with something. It is time to turn off all the "noise" and get rid of all the clutter that is suffocating the beauty of living.

"The Internet allows the small guy a global marketplace. But technology is harmful in the sense that we get too much information from it. Because of the web we get 10 times the amount of noise we ever got, which makes harmful fallacies far more likely."

- Nassim Nicholas Taleb

Taking back this valuable ground is **our** responsibility, not Mark Zuckerberg's or Jack Dorsey's. They didn't do anything wrong, they merely created tools that we can use. It is we who have obsessed with them and allowed them to rule our lives. Carefully and wisely managed, they can be very useful tools but few people are disciplined enough to turn them off when necessary. It's your choice but as for me, I am doing my best to get some "sweet doing nothing" back into my life!

How to cultivate *dolce far niente*:

Turn off the TV, computer or phone
Yes, they have off buttons! No, they are not connected to your oxygen supply so you won't die when they are switched off! There is a whole beautiful world out there that we more often only see through sunsets shared on our friends' Facebook pages. We talk a big game on Twitter but how many of us manage to get to places where there is no reception to tweet? When last did

you simply sit in the garden and see how many bird visitors you have? Do you remember the last time you took a stroll to nowhere in particular for no real reason, simply to see what you could see? Do you take your mobile phone with you on family holidays or do you leave it at home? Try to do things differently when it comes to technology, experiment a little and see how it impacts yours and your family's lives. To be honest, we don't need to see another person's dinner on Instragram anymore. Do we need to see every single family outing of every single family we have on Facebook? Will we miss anything if we don't see the latest rant on Twitter? Life is passing us by; slow it down a little by dotting moments of sweet nothing into your days.

Sit outside and simply watch the world go by

Before I got distracted by technology I used to quite enjoy sitting in a coffee shop and watch the people pass by. I also used to enjoy sitting on the rocks at the beach watching the waves crash violently against them. I remember gazing out of the living room window at the wind blowing in the trees, leaves falling and snow drifting through the air in winter. On one particular midnight I happened to notice how amazing the moon looked hanging in a very dramatic sky and so I went outside in my pyjamas and sat on a bench to gaze at it for what must have been a full hour or more. I say all this in past tense because it has been a while since I have taken time to watch the world go by and fully intend to get back to it as a matter of urgency! I also intend to teach my children to slow down too as they are very quickly getting into the terrible technology trap! My six year old can figure out a new device quicker than I can and my eight year old is teaching me new things on his tablet. How and when did this happen? I certainly didn't teach them how to use these devices! I also didn't buy him the tablet, a well-meaning family member did and now I have to deal with it. Be careful what you allow around little ones – just saying... It's not that technology is bad, it is great, however anything without boundaries can be dangerous and too much of a good thing can be a bad thing.

Listen ... REALLY listen ... to your loved ones.

The evils of multi-tasking has meant that we only half listen to people. By doing this we are sending out a message that they are not important, that what they are saying is not important and that we have more important things to do. Not only do we not truly hear what they have to say and miss out on vital clues to their problems and joys but we also send them a consistent message that will hurt them. When someone speaks to you, give them your full attention and communicate that you love and care for them; in a work situation really listen to communicate respect. If it is genuinely a bad time and you cannot give them that attention then let them know and give them a time when you will be free to do so rather than half listen or completely blank them. Remember, people are very important.

Take it one step further and do sweet nothing with your loved ones. I have a sofa in my office and sometimes one of the children come home from school with seemingly nothing to say and will hover around my desk. When possible, I take them to my sofa and sit them on my lap and have a silent cuddle. It's ok not to talk sometimes. Even children like to just be silent at times. When we sit and cuddle, either something that is bothering them comes out when they start to talk, or they get filled up with love and are happy to leave my office and go play until dinner time. Either way, it is always well worth taking a few minutes away from work to totally focus on my children!

Watch your children play

There is so much to learn from child's play. Not only to learn but also simply to enjoy. I have had many pleasurable moments from watching the children play when they don't realise that I am watching them. It gives me time to observe who they really are; discover new things about them and even see little character flaws that need to be addressed. On the flip side, as I watch my children I learn a lot about myself as they often act as little mirrors of truth.

"As I watch my children I learn a lot about myself as they often act as little mirrors of truth."

I see my own character flaws when I observe them play, I see how they treat people and consider if I treat people in the same way. It's not all negative though; I often see great confirmation of the things I get right too as they copy both the good and bad things – they don't know the difference, they simply trust that their parents must know what they are doing so it's safe to copy.

Eat slowly and chat at meal times

I am so guilty of rushing meal times. Firstly because it is the end of the day and I am usually tired and stressed – again not something I am proud of but one I am working on. Secondly because the children eat very slowly, meal times can take an hour as they laugh, chat, play and eat! The worst part is that they are right and I am wrong! Meal times should take an hour and involve socialising as a family. It should not be a rush job that we check off on our "to do" list before we move onto the next item on the agenda. Evening meal times are a great way to turn off from the day's work and focus on more relaxing evening activities. I would often go back to my office and work after putting my children to bed as I enjoyed the silence and found this time to be my most productive. However, this shouldn't mean that I rush through meal times to get back to work. So what I prefer to do now is to only work occasionally in the evenings and mostly focus on relaxation or writing instead (which is very relaxing for me).

Take your time, stop rushing.

Rather than seeing each and every task that you have to do each day as something that *has* to be done, why not enjoy everything that you *get* to do? It's a wonderful exercise of gratitude more than anything. For example, rather than saying that you *have to* drive your children to school why not say that you *get to* drive them to school? See the privilege in what you have to do, make the time with them count on each and every car journey. Play games, sing songs or just chat about the day ahead or the day they are coming home from. Always remind yourself that there are people who struggle to conceive and don't have the privilege of having children or people who have lost a child to some tragedy and would give anything to be able to drive their children to school once again.

Instead of saying, I *have* to go to work, why not say I *get* to go to work and am so grateful as there are many people in this world who would love to have a job to go to.

This exercise can be applied to any and every task that you have to do each and every day. You can even apply it to washing the dishes as you think of the millions of people out there that do not have clean running water. If it doesn't tug at your heart strings, turn off your main water supply for two days and find alternative ways to get by. In fact I have just decided that at least once a year we should do this in our home so that we never take our privileged life for granted. Slow down and take time to enjoy them all. What is the rush anyway?

Leave gaps in your schedule

Stop packing things next to each other so tightly in your diary. Give yourself space to breathe. I discovered how guilty I was of packing things extremely tightly into my diary when on several occasions I realised that I forgot to factor in one, sometimes even two, meals into my day. On one occasion I felt extremely ill as I had forgotten to factor in lunch and dinner but went onto an evening cocktails and canapés event! Needless to say the food and drink didn't sit well in my stomach. Back to back meetings still occur from time to time in my schedule as it allows me to save travel time by seeing a few people one after the other. However these days are the exception not the norm anymore. I have since learned that if I have a meeting near to a beautiful park I should allow time to have a walk in it, and if I have to travel somewhere new, to allow time to do some sightseeing.

"Your time is limited, so don't waste it living someone else's life. Don't be trapped by dogma - which is living with the results of other people's thinking. Don't let the noise of others' opinions drown out your own inner voice."

- Steve Jobs

What's your bath?

OK, so I did it in the bath. I also do it sitting by the pond in my garden, having coffee with my daughter, playing my guitar or piano, singing loudly and out of tune in my car and by walking to the top of the hill near our home and marvelling at creation. All these things can occur during my working week because I know that doing them is good for my business. Staying inspired is essential to my business and I cannot be inspired sitting in front of a computer all day. I do spend a lot of time with people teaching and training but I am an introvert so even though I love it, it is something that drains me.

You may say I did it in the dance studio or with a pot of paints. Some of you may say that you did it on your motorbike or while belly dancing. The whole point is to find out what inspires you, what keeps you motivated and what makes the journey enjoyable. Taking time out to think is not only acceptable in any business day but is actually essential!

I Did it Consistently

"Act as if what you do makes a difference. It does.."

- William James

Success is doing the same thing for a long period of time.

Repetition pays. It really is that simple. Keep doing the same thing consistently, getting better at it each time until you wake up and realise that you have succeeded in what you set out to do. There may be tweaks needed along the way, especially if you are looking for a different outcome. Then you have to do the same thing but in many different ways. There is no point doing the same thing repeatedly and expecting different results. However, if it works on a small scale keep repeating it until it grows and grows.

"The definition of insanity is doing something over and over again and expecting a different result."

- Author Unknown

Let me give you an example of one of the most boring and mundane things that I had to do for years to get the Women's Business Club to where it is today. Most days I would spend hours on Facebook, Twitter, LinkedIn and Google + finding my target audience, connecting with them, introducing myself, having a chat and adding them to my database. The way I see it is that there are literally billions of my target audience at my fingertips but I had to do the boring, hard work of connecting with them. My goal was not

117

just to collect data but to connect with them too so my next task was to have lots of cups of coffee with lots of people. Year one produced a very high coffee expenditure in my financial report but it was worth it. My very first Women's Business Club was built on about 90% of my social media contacts. Each and every club has been started in the same way and some franchisees actually left us when they realised how much boring hard work went into pulling an event off. It seems that everyone loves Women's Business Club and wants to be involved until they realise that it takes a lot of work to be successful. They see the results and want to experience results but don't see all the boring behind the scenes stuff that goes on to make it work!

Another boring and repetitive thing that we do is we track everything. We test and measure each and every marketing effort. Every email gets logged, every phone calls gets logged, our social media activity is monitored and we do our best to see what is working and what is not. One of the results was our zero advertising policy. We measured our response from various paid advertising methods and came to the conclusion that our company does not work this way. Relationship and personal connection is what works for us. So we consistently build our company through the one on one personal connection. If we had not tested and measured everything we could have wasted thousands in advertising. Our preferred budget is in coffees and meals. We like to meet people!

Remember, something might become boring and old to you but there are thousands of people that have yet to hear of it, so keep plugging away consistently until the majority of people have heard of what you are trying to promote. If it works keep doing it over and over and over again. If it doesn't work tweak over and over and over again until it does work. From time to time trust your gut instinct and pull the plug on the things that are not working at all.

Practice Makes Perfect

There is much debate about whether Malcolm Gladwell's thesis that it takes 10,000 hours to learn a new skill is correct. In Gladwell's book, *Outliers*, he claims that the key to success in any field is, to a large extent, a matter of practicing a specific task for a total of around 10,000 hours. Josh Kaufman, the author of *The Personal MBA: Master the Art of Business* and *The First 20 Hours: How to Learn Anything... Fast!* says that it takes 20 hours and not 10,000 hours to learn a skill. Daniel Goleman, in his book, *Focus: The Hidden Driver of Excellence* says that *"The '10,000-hour rule' – that this level of practice holds the secret to great success in any field – has become sacrosanct gospel, echoed on websites and recited as litany in high-performance workshops. The problem: it's only half-true. If you are a duffer at golf, say, and make the same mistakes every time you try a certain swing or putt, 10,000 hours of practicing that error will not improve your game. You'll still be a duffer, albeit an older one."*

What do you say? I say that practice does make perfect but it needs to include other factors too. Practicing the *wrong* thing or the wrong technique for 10,000 hours might mean that you end up with some very bad habits. This sort of practice will never make perfect, so just pure practice without any guidance or measures can be very dangerous; you could just end up being extremely bad at something! Back to Daniel Goleman who referred to his concept of *smart practice* when he said: *"(The experts) concentrate actively on those moves they have yet to perfect, on correcting what's not working in their game, and on refining their mental models of how to play the game. The secret to smart practice boils down to focus on the particulars of feedback from a seasoned coach."*

The bottom line is that practice is important but there is so much more that needs to be included when practicing. One of the key elements is who you get your feedback from and we will cover that in depth in the next chapter. Hard work and lots of practice is essential but working smart and practicing the right thing is the key.

What Does Your Gut Say?

Is Gladwell correct? Is what I say in this book correct? I believe that we all get a piece of the puzzle in this life and not the whole puzzle. As we read books, talk to people and study to become better at what we do in this life we need to mostly rely on our gut instinct.

Do What Consistently?

It's easy to say do it consistently, but what exactly should be done consistently in business? There are some vital things that should be done consistently and some equally important things that should not be done consistently. Let's take a look at them now.

DO consistently:

DO daily marketing

Marketing underpins your business and should be done daily. Consistent marketing will lead to consistent sales. Ideally you should have 20 to 30 channels to market and working them takes a lot of time. Too often people dabble with one or two marketing activities, don't see instant results and then move on. Your marketing will only yield the results you desire if you stick at it consistently. In this day and age we have very many free marketing options that can be used very effectively such as social media, email marketing, etc. We also need to include some good old fashioned phone calls and snail mail letters too. A good variety of consistent marketing activity is guaranteed to grow any business if you get the three M's right. Your M's are your Market, Message and Media. Let's break them down and really focus so that you can consistently do the sort of marketing that will be most effective.

M = Market

This is *who* you are selling too. More often than not when I ask any business owner who their target audience is they say everyone! I always respond with, "Everyone is no one!" and what I mean by that is that everyone is too general. It's like trying to shoot something small like a mouse in a field of long grass with a shot gun. It's unlikely that you will hit the target. To be effective in your marketing you really need to find out who needs what you have to offer. Another big mistake I have come across is people assuming that everyone wants what they have to offer. Again, that is a terrible assumption and if you don't do your research and find out what your target market really wants then your marketing will fail.

So to sum it up, who is your target market? What do they need from you? What is their pain? What keeps them up at night worrying? What problem can you solve for them? What benefits do your products or services offer them? Answer all these questions and you will quickly find your market.

M = Message

What do you need to say to your market to get them interested in your product or service? This is your message. The best messages are the ones that evoke emotions in some way. A message that makes you feel something is a powerful message. What does your target market need and how does having it make them feel? Help those who need what you have to offer feel good about coming to you for it.

M = Media

Finally, you need to choose the type of marketing media that suits your market and message. If you are marketing to retirees then using social media may not be the best medium and if you are marketing to young women in their twenties then social media will definitely be your best bet.

Yesterday my daughter posted a message about some marketing material that she received through her letterbox. It was from a landscaping company. She lives in an apartment on the third floor. The message and media may have been spot on but it was delivered to the wrong market! People in apartments don't need info about having the perfect lawn. What a waste of expensive marketing material.

DO treat people well

People buy from people. If someone likes you or the person that they encounter in your business they might buy from you but if they don't like the person representing your business they won't. It's that simple. Ensure that you are consistently treating people well and training your team to do the same. You cannot go wrong by making people feel good about themselves. You have the power to do this simply by treating them with respect and kindness. How you treat people should never depend on how you feel but on how you want them to feel.

DO keep a cash backup

I may have said this one too many times but cash is king! Consistently build your cash reserves so that you never find yourself in the unfortunate position of running out of money. If you consistently put a percentage of your profits away for a rainy day you will never be caught out.

DO suffer a short term sacrifice for long term gain

Chris Gardner's story became well known when it was turned into a Hollywood movie called *The Pursuit of Happiness* with Will Smith as Gardner, an on-and-off-homeless salesman. Although Chris Gardner did at one point have money, he invested it unwisely and lost it all, leading him to spend a year on the streets, destitute and homeless. From this hopeless place he succeeded in setting up his own hugely successful multimillion-dollar institutional investment firm. Fascinated by finance, but without connections and a suitable education, Gardner had the audacity to apply for a training program at a brokerage, willing to live on the street with no income to help him achieve his goal. I can only imagine that anyone who had known him would have questioned his seemingly irrational decision, but Gardner knew exactly what he wanted and was willing to pay whatever price he needed to pay for his success. He had nothing but a goal. How badly

I Did it in My Pyjamas

do you want your business to work and what are you willing to do or sacrifice to make it happen?

DO test and measure everything before you invest
Here are 5 basic steps on how to do this:

1. Backup

Don't risk more than you are willing to lose. Create a backup that will sustain you should your experiment fail. It's one thing taking a risk but it is another taking a calculated risk. My first business failed because I risked all with no backup. I have since learned the importance of a backup. It's not rocket science, if you are going to do anything major on your computer you first create a backup, if you are writing a book you will back up your work regularly.

2. Test

Now that you have your safety net in place, take a reasonable amount of money to conduct your experiment. Don't play with more than you are willing to lose because the chances are you will lose a few times before you gain. My first experiment was to *play* on the stock market... I have yet to recover but am still learning. I also experimented with various forms of advertising which resulted in a significant loss of money and a clear zero advertising policy in our company handbook. Some testing involved buying and selling certain products and other testing involved taking a risk on particular people. To date I have been burned more times that I have succeeded with all of the above, however I am still in business as my backup kept our company afloat.

3. Measure

Knowing whether or not your experiment worked will be based on the recorded results. There is so much to be learned for those who want to learn but for those who just want to make money so much is lost. The difference between the two can be put down to how much you choose to see and how much you write down.

At Women's Business Club we write down any and every form of marketing into a spreadsheet. Each and every client has a marketing box allocated to them in our database so we can be sure how they found out about us. We punch all the numbers into our spreadsheet and can quickly measure what form of marketing is working and what is not.

The same can be applied to time and money. We ask ourselves regularly, what did we spend our time and money on, what were the results and based on the data we either invest more into our particular efforts or scrap them entirely. The key is knowing your numbers. You cannot make *inform*ed decisions without *inform*ation.

4. Back up

Once you have tested and measured take some time to build up your backup before trying again.

5. Try Again

Once you have recuperated your backup fund, try again. Try and try until you succeed. Each time you give it another go make sure that you have learned from your previous attempt and that you enjoy the journey going forward.

DO NOT do consistently:

Here are some equally important things that you should not do consistently.

DO NOT repeat the same mistakes

Failure is good! I wholeheartedly believe that there is no such thing as success without failure. However, failing at the same thing repeatedly because you keep doing the same thing is silly. Sure, fail, give anything a go, but when you try again do things differently until you succeed. Don't expect different results from repeatedly doing that same thing. Assess what you are doing on a regular basis so that you can be clear about what is working and what is not.

DO NOT spend more than you earn

Guess what, if you consistently spend more than you earn you will very quickly run out of money. Now one thing is crucial – cash is king and if you are consistently making no money in your business then you do need to rethink things. No matter what anyone says or how good you are at what you do, the fact is that NO SALES = NO BUSINESS. Cash flow is everything in business. The difference between a great hobby and a great business is the amount of income it generates. Yes, a hobby can turn into a business but without profit you don't have a business. "Sales" doesn't necessary come naturally to all entrepreneurs but the ability to sell your product or service is essential to all entrepreneurs. If you find that you struggle in this area do something about it. Read sales books, attend seminars, ask others who are good at it for tips and try one or two things out for yourself to see what feels best for you. The bottom line is that saying that you are no good at sales in not a good excuse: you have to be brilliant at sales if you want to build a great business.

Once you have made money, no matter how much or how little, it is essential to know what to do with it. Some people achieve *phase one* which is making money but then never get beyond this phase and end up living in a vicious cycle of making enough money to stay afloat. Sadly their expenses begin to exceed their income and the business fails.

The key to breaking through to the next level is experimenting. Find your own ways to take the little that you have and grow it into more. Too many business owners never achieve financial freedom because they enjoy the little money that they do make and spend it as opposed to invest it so that it grows. There is no recipe for how to make *your* money grow, you will need to figure that out for yourself and for your business. Testing and measuring is the sure way to find your way forward.

A true entrepreneur will not be content putting their money into a savings account or handing it over to a professional investor. An entrepreneur likes to play with his money and watch it grow.

"A true entrepreneur will not be content putting their money into a savings account or handing it over to a professional investor. An entrepreneur likes to play with his money and watch it grow."

Where necessary they will take risks but if they are wise they will keep enough backup money so that the risk won't cause their business to go under. I took many risks in my first business venture but I did not have any backup cash, so the risk not only cost me my business but also left me paying off the debt it caused over the ten years that followed. I have since learned the value of having some money to play with while keeping enough backed up should my playing go wrong.   I believe an entrepreneur isn't satisfied by money itself but their pleasure comes from making it grow and the most satisfied of all entrepreneurs are the ones who enjoy giving it away too, but that is another chapter.

I Did it with Five People

"You are the average of the five people you spend the most time with."

- Jim Rohn

You can choose your friends.

*M*y friendships are very important to me but I don't have many of them. Yes I *know* hundreds of women all over the country and I get to network with many amazing women. These woman dip in and dip out of my life, they help me and I help them when necessary or we simply enjoy each other's company. I feel blessed to know so many amazing women and I would not have the amazing business I have today if it weren't for every one of them and the good and bad experiences we have had together. The Women's Business Club is built on people and exists for people, so it stands to reason that people are very important to me.

I am the sort of person that is an open book. I have no problem sharing any part of my life story whenever relevant. In fact I have written 27 books sharing my life and experiences and I never have to worry that a deep dark secret will one day be uncovered because I have been transparent about my life every step of the way. However, there are few people that I know, who know me well enough, to offer me the right advice and support in my business. These few people usually amount to no more than five at any point in my life – and five is about all you need. Maintaining a healthy, deep relationship takes a lot of time, you can't *really* get to know someone in a Facebook chat box or by seeing them once a month for coffee. My good friends are people who I have spent many hours with both on good days and on bad days. They really know me, they have seen me at my best and at my worst and have stuck around. My loyalty and respect for these friends run deep and there is pretty much nothing I would not do for them and I believe they feel the same way about me. We have chosen each other to be friends and we have invested in our friendship over the years.

Champions and Cheerleaders

The five people you spend the most time with will be the greatest influence in your life and in your business. Choosing the best five people to spend time with is essential to success in this life. These are the people in your life who are thoroughly positive and will champion your cause or be your personal cheerleaders. Finding these five is not as easy as it sounds. Unfortunately most people are too selfish to be someone else's cheerleader or too insecure to champion someone else's cause. My main cheerleaders are my husband, my mother and my daughter. I don't know what I would do without the three of them. They always believe in me, always have my back but love me enough to tell me the hard truths when I need to hear them. They are my champions who believe in me. Without them I could not have come this far. If I have a down day they remind me of why I do what I do, if I stop believing in myself they affirm me and remind me of who I really am. I can't imagine my life without my family and they are people who I cannot spend enough time with – time with them is *never* a waste of time. I am truly blessed to have these three as well as the rest of my family who are just as supportive.

The other two of my five seem to be changing lately but have been equally important in my journey so far. Seasons change and it is normal that people come and go. Some of my good friends live several hours away from where I live. We used to live nearby and spent many hours getting to know each other but now that we have moved apart we don't get to see each other as much. We still keep in touch and each time we see each other we have a lot to say and catch up on. It's wonderful to be able to just pick up where we left off last time – 10 years have passed in some cases but our friendships have continued to blossom over this time.

However, the season has changed and these friends are less involved in the day to day running of my life and business. I have specifically chosen two other women who I "give" myself and my time to and who I trust with my life. I have taken time to build friendships with them because I look up to them and I know that they will tell me the truth, even if I don't like what they have to say. This is priceless, a good friend who is not scared to hurt you for the right reasons is a treasure. Many say what they think you want to hear or even flatter you, but those who are honest no matter what the cost are friends to keep close.

One such friend was the making of me, she really was. Her name is Jill Chitty and she is a fantastic marketing coach and business mentor, and the founder of Grow Unlimited. In fact I very much attribute the start of my journey to the Women's Business Club to her. When I was in a teary mess, she said one sentence that set me up for life! She said, "But Angela, I see you as a business woman." You see, I was doubting myself and had no clue that I had anything to offer the business world. My husband, daughter and mother were always affirming me but I was so used to it that it didn't have the same impact as the words of this woman did. She was a successful business woman who I deeply admired. I learned so much from and her comment really hit me where I needed it most. Just knowing that someone like her saw me as a peer changed everything. This is why we need friends and if we don't invest in our friendships then we eliminate room for such life changing encounters to occur.

Jill was a good friend to me in a season where I really needed her. We didn't stop being friends, nothing happened and we didn't fall out or have a disagreement, we simply grew apart and stopped spending as much time together as our needs and life changed. I still consider Jill an amazing friend but we are no longer a part of each other's five. She has new influencers now and so do I. We are both doing well in our chosen paths and from time to time cross paths at various events. It's always wonderful to see Jill and to catch up.

There was a time when life was really tough personally. Our son was diagnosed with diabetes, we had a failed attempt at building a church and had to recover financially from years of unpaid work and much more, so much more. It really was a trying few years which wore me down more than I realised. Earlier, under the chapter "I Did it with Depression", I shared the story about the night when I was due to speak at the Chamber of Commerce but on my way there while I stopped to drop off the children at my friend's home I simply fell apart. That was the evening that my good friend Fay was brave enough to tell me the truth – that I was overworked, depressed and needed to stop. I honestly don't know what would have happened to me if it weren't for her. She has definitely been one of my five, not as a business mentor but as one who genuinely cares about me and looks out for me as I do for her. She noticed the signs and saw that was burned out and spiralling into a deep depression. Coping was what I had learned to do and I was living in survival mode, but Faye knew me well enough and saw me often enough to know that something was not right. She quite possibly saved my life! As a result I was able to take stock, slow down and rebuild myself from a very broken state. Good friends are hard to find but I seem to be blessed with really amazing ones. Faye and I were very close but now see less of each other even though we live in the same neighbourhood. It's not that anything bad happened but simply that life happened. She was obviously exactly who I needed for that season of my life. We both invested a lot in our friendship and became close. Even though we see each other less frequently now I know that should either one of us need each other we would drop everything to do whatever is needed. We will always be friends but we won't always be in each other's five.

As a result I'm currently on the lookout for the right people to replace the two that have moved out of my life so I can maintain the right balance in the people I have around me. Right now, I need women in my life who are ahead of me in the game. I am keen to learn and glean from successful business women. I can feel that I am ready for another growth spurt and I know I need someone who will stretch me and challenge me. I have a "vacancy" in my five and am strategically and intentionally looking for the right two people who will allow me into their life.

Sometimes you meet the right people effortlessly and at other times you have to search them out. I remember a similar time, over ten years ago now, when I did just this. I recognised two women who I really wanted to learn from. They were amazing and inspired me greatly. Rather than asking them for their time I decided to get into their world by offering value to them instead. It sounds incredibly strategic and it was. I simply emailed Joyce and asked her what I could do to serve her. I told her my particular skill set and asked if she had any need of any of my skills and ended off by saying that I was willing to do anything to serve her. Knowing that she had just moved home I offered to help with her unpacking and she accepted. I not only spend some lovely time with her unpacking her children's clothing into the cupboard but I went on to sorting out her filing system for her property business. She was stunned at what I achieved for her, saying, "Angela you have opened my eyes!" I was able to show her a different way to manage her properties that was much more efficient. Why did I volunteer my time like that to do such menial tasks? I did it because I recognised that I wanted her to be in my five for that season but I didn't want to be a burden to her. The result was a wonderful relationship and although it was a short season she knows who I am and I can call on her anytime for advice or referrals. She is a wonderful inspiration to many women and I count it a privilege to have learned from her.

In my search for the right people to have around me there are some amazing women I have approached but they are too busy. There are some I would just like to make tea for so I can learn from them but alas they have said no. So I continue to look for and reach out to people until I find a match. My intention is not to be a leech or a crab but to learn and to give back where I can. The bottom line is that I know that I need inspiring people in my life so that I can learn and grow. It would be foolish for me to even consider trying to do life and business on my own without any influence, support or criticism. Every single person I come into contact with, even the negative, hurtful ones, can help me on my path. However, we still need to be cautious when it comes to those who could really harm our progress. We must limit the time we spend around them.

Crabs in a Bucket

Crab mentality is a phrase that describes a way of thinking best described by the phrase, "If I can't have it, neither can you." These are the types of people who can't get ahead and won't allow anyone else to either. The metaphor refers to a pot of crabs. Individually, the crabs could easily escape from the pot, but instead, they grab at each other in a useless "king of the hill" competition which prevents any from escaping and ensures their collective demise. The analogy in human behaviour is sometimes claimed to be that members of a group will attempt to "pull down" anyone who achieves success beyond the others, out of envy, conspiracy or competitive feelings. This term is broadly associated with short-sighted, non-constructive thinking rather than a unified, long-term, constructive mentality that research has shown can result in a reduction of average performance by around 20%. While the reason for crab mentality is claimed to be jealousy, and a behavioural trait indulged in despite people knowing it to be disadvantageous to them, it can also arise from a paucity of resources leading to perpetual competition.

So the big question is, who are the crabs in your life? Who is pulling you down at every opportunity, discouraging you on your path and telling you that you cannot do it? Nine times out of ten these people are jealous or simply too lazy to be bothered to attempt anything ambitious themselves or feel like a failure so want you to fail too. Sometimes they simply don't even realise that they are crabs or don't have the faith and vision that you have. Either way, you cannot let these crabs hold onto you and bring you down, you must pull away from them and allow them limited or if possible no contact with you.

7 steps for dealing with people who bring you down

Over the years I have learned many valuable lessons and one of them is that I don't have to listen to or read everything that everyone says about me. The first time I got a bad book review I felt like my whole world had crashed.

Perhaps the review was true or perhaps it was not, but I have since learned that there will never be 100% positive reviews for everything that I do.

I have also learned how to very succinctly and diplomatically respond to very long accusatory emails. Nine times out of ten I will simply reply, "I am sorry you feel that way. Have a lovely day. Kind Regards, Angela." Now of course, some emails deserve a good thorough response or a phone call, and I have made some of those lately. However, when people are out to attack me for no real reason, based on gossip or lies, I have learned to use my polite, short response.

"Save your skin from the corrosive acids from the mouths of toxic people. Someone who just helped you to speak evil about another person can later help another person to speak evil about you."

- Israelmore Ayivor

Equally, I have had to learn over the years to bite my tongue and not react to things that people say. Instead, I respond. The words may sound similar but their effect is vastly different. Reacting is always an emotional response whereas responding is more logical. Reacting is what gets people into trouble as they don't take time to think about what they are saying and may regret it later. Responding is a well thought out response without the emotional stabbing that yields the best results.

So both written and verbal, I have learned but not yet mastered, how to deal with people who bring me down. So here are my 7 steps for dealing with people who bring you down:

Step 1: Assess

People who bring you down are often like poison slowly entering your blood stream without you realising it. Family, friends and others close to you will have this affect as you see them often and don't even realise that they are affecting you at all.

The second type of person who brings you down is the type of person who doesn't know you well at all and just takes "stabs" at you with nasty words or even worse, gossip behind your back.

Taking care of yourself involves assessing the people who affect you, how they affect you and why they affect you. Assess how you feel about them and also how you feel about the way they make you feel. Take stock and try to remain as unemotional as possible.

My biggest weakness is blaming myself, if someone brings me down I consider whether or not they are saying is accurate and usually find a reason why I am to blame. This has been exhausting over the years and I am pleased to report that I am getting much better at blaming myself a lot less.

Step 2: Understand

Before jumping to conclusions, try to understand what exactly is causing your friend, client or colleague's behaviour. Are they perhaps feeling insecure around you or intimidated by you? Have they perhaps had some bad information that they are believing to be true? Seek truth first. Sometimes people don't bring you down on purpose and with a little understanding and communication you can end up with a stronger and more positive relationship than before.

Recently I had a situation in our Women's Business Club when one of our team left the company and sadly rumours spread about me which resulted in a mass exodus of members. It was heart-breaking and what I hated most was that the rumours were all completely false – made up stories that were destroying me. I almost thought I would lose my company as a result of the damage. So what I did was to make contact with each and every member of that club and ask to have a chat with them. The response was very mixed, some agreed, some ignored me completely and others took it

I Did it in My Pyjamas

upon themselves to be very nasty. I did my best to understand their position, which was largely a belief of untruths that were told about me. I also hoped to explain my side of the story so that they could have a better understanding of the truth.

Step 3: Decide

The difficult part is to know which relationships are worth your time and investment and which ones you need to cut loose. Of course there are times when you *are* the problem and need to apologise. In the case of some of the members who were willing to meet up with me, I made a point of apologising for the misunderstanding or whatever else I could think of apologising for. I clearly explained the truth and I could see that they genuinely understood the truth. They decided to stay as a result.

But now let's look at the other ones who were purely nasty for reasons that I do not know and cannot understand. In these cases I made a clear and firm decision to cut them loose. What these people chose to believe and do was out of my control and there was nothing that I could do about it – so I decided to distance myself from them for my own good. It would have been a waste of time for me to try and convince them to meet with me or even read an email from me as they had already made up their mind about what they believed to be true. It was sad but I decided that it was best to let them go.

Your situation may not be a business one. If it is a family member that is bringing you down then you need to make a firm decision to spend less time with them. If it is a work colleague then deal with them professionally and if it is someone who you don't need to see or talk to then why not just cut them loose? You have the power of decision when it comes to people and how much you allow them to affect you. You don't have to spend time with the people that bring you down, it is your decision.

Step 4: Commit

There is nothing worse than when a couple break up, make up and break up repeatedly. It only ever ends in disaster and heartache. If you have decided to cut ties with the people that bring you down then commit to your decision. Don't feel sorry for them or give them one more chance. It's not to say that they may not change in the future and find their way back into your life but if they are bringing you down and you have decided that you don't want to spend time with them, then commit to your decision. You will only do yourself harm by not setting boundaries with negative people and people who bring you down.

Step 5: Let Go

Easier said than done, but after committing you need to let go. In the case of my club that went wrong, I had to let go of each person. I had several thriving clubs at the time and if I spent all my energy trying to hold onto the very people that were bringing me down then I would have neglected all our other members in the other clubs.

Similarly, in a family situation, if we don't let go of the family member who brings us down then we may miss out on experiencing a wonderful and positive relationship with our other family members.

Letting go doesn't mean giving up on people, it simply means that you are not willing to allow them to bring you down anymore and will do whatever is necessary to let go. We can always hope and believe that people will change but we don't need to allow ourselves to be their punching bag while they do so.

Step 6: Reaffirm Yourself

Often after being through a difficult patch with people we can experience a knock in our confidence and identity. It is important after letting go to have some time to heal. When my team member left the company I would wake up crying most mornings as I was really fond of her. It occurred to me after a few days that I was actually grieving. I was very surprised to have had such a strong reaction but it also affirmed that I really do care for my team like my own family so losing one of them is always going to be traumatic. I know people will come and go in the Women's Business Club. I have no complaints about her and as far as I know she has no complaints about me, it was simply her time to move on.

However, the members who left were the ones who did the most damage based on the nonsense they believed. They said some pretty nasty things to me and I needed to take some time out to reaffirm my identity. I had to tell myself that I was not who they said I am. They have never met me and do not know me. I know who I am and am constantly working on being a better person.

I gave myself this little speech and took time to remember the truth about me so that the lies that were told would lose their power. Sadly, we will all have to go through this from time to time in life. There will always be people that will bring us down for whatever reason but we must not allow them to affect our confidence and identity.

Step 7: Find Positive People

After some weeks had passed I approached a wonderful lady in our VIP Club and asked her if we could spend some time together on a regular basis so I could bounce some ideas off her and she off me should she wish to. She is a lovely, friendly and positive woman who is successful in life and business. Like me, she is also a mother so I felt that we could understand each other well. It was essential for me to move on by finding positive people to spend time with.

The great thing about spending time with the right people is that they will tell you the truth but won't bring you down when doing so. I cannot stress enough the importance of having such people in your life. You don't want flatterers or people that will pat you on the back and say whatever you need to hear all the time. A good positive person who will tell you the truth when you need it hear it is invaluable. Once you have let go of the negative people and reaffirmed yourself, ensure that you have some lovely positive people to surround yourself with.

Being One of Five

It's one thing looking for five amazing people to do life with but are you willing to be a part of someone else's five? Is there someone who is not as far along in the journey as you who could really use your attention from time to time? Are you willing to give a little time and attention to a start up in business or a young mother having her first child? What you sow you reap and if you are struggling to find someone to be one of your five perhaps you need to sow a little kindness first.

"A real friend is one who walks in when the rest of the world walks out."

- Walter Winchell

Who is walking into your life when everyone else is leaving you stranded? Whose life do you need to walk into right now? Pay attention to the people in your world as businesses and lives are built on people.

I Did it Despite Opposition

"A successful man is one who can lay a firm foundation with the bricks others have thrown at him."

- David Brinkley

What doesn't kill you makes you stronger.

It wouldn't be a complete book if we didn't delve into the really difficult stuff. This is the stuff that make or break the best of us. Most of us need to be liked, in fact I don't think anyone *likes* being disliked. There are varying levels of opposition from being disliked to being violently opposed. Each of us have to face all degrees but few make it as it's tough even for the thickest skinned people!

"Success is not measured by what you accomplish, but by the opposition you have encountered, and the courage with which you have maintained the struggle against overwhelming odds."

- Orison Swett Marden

Let me share some of my stories with you, some still open wounds that will take time to heal. In the first year of the Women's Business Club I enjoyed helping women with their businesses and saw some great results. I did so for little or no profit as I felt I had to prove myself in the business world. To be honest I wasn't very confident so really it was mostly a case of proving to myself that I really did have something to offer others. Everything went swimmingly well and I started to see some fantastic results. One lady in particular came to me for just about everything and I happily helped her for the reward of seeing her grow and succeed. I became very fond of her so didn't charge much and at times she even paid me in her beauty products rather than real money. I didn't really need the products but was happy to be helping her.

Time passed and I watched her grow and flourish then she stopped needing me. In time she pretty much cut me off and starting going to someone else for help. She paid this other lady for help. This stung a little. It wasn't long before she didn't have anything good to say about me, in fact negativity about me leaked through the business network. For some reason it seemed that she had forgotten everything that I had done for her and chose to focus on one or two things she disliked about me and the way I was running my business. Needless to say this hurt a great deal. I really wanted her to like me and to tell others about how much I had helped her so that they would come to me for help too. Eventually I gave up when I realised that I could spend a lot of time trying to win her favour and despite my best efforts never succeed. So in order to save time and money, I decided to let her go. It broke my heart because I was very fond of her and believed in her potential. I found it difficult to let go and move on but I knew I had to. So I did. Even writing about it now does hurt a little, deep down inside I would still like her to like me. I had to forgive her so that my heart wouldn't get bitter but I also had to learn to grow a thick skin – not everyone will like me.

You can't please everyone

So this was my first valuable lesson in opposition, no matter how much I want to please everyone, I simply can't! And so I learned a few truths about myself and people:

- People see you through their own filtering system. You cannot change how they see you.
- Some people can't be pleased no matter how hard you try. It is their problem not yours.
- People's opinion of you doesn't make it truth – it is only their opinion.

- You need to know yourself well enough to know what is true and what is not. Work on your faults and shrug off what is not true.
- People will try pull you down because they are jealous; feel pity for them but don't allow them to pull you down.
- Strive to have a thick skin and a soft heart.
- Forgive everyone always. Forgive doesn't mean forget.

People pleasing is actually a sign of weakness I have discovered. The first level of strength in business comes when you can get past people pleasing and focus on building a business with the understanding that not everyone will like you and agree with you. It's tough but this is the truth. Unfortunately if you are a people pleaser you are likely to be putting everyone else's needs ahead of your own, which means that you are not doing a very good job of building your business or your life. Here are my top tips to stop people pleasing:

Accept yourself

You cannot deal with people pleasing if you are not confident in who you are – the good, the bad and the ugly. I have spent years learning to accept myself, to know my strengths as well as my weaknesses. I use my strengths, I accept my weaknesses and I work on my character flaws. I constantly strive to grow and become a better person but I cannot be strong at everything, so I accept what I can and can't do which makes it so much easier to set boundaries.

Set boundaries

Boundaries help you and other people know what they can expect from you personally and from your business. Boundaries say you can come this far and no further or that you will go this far and no further. For me boundaries had to be set in my pricing structure with a clear message of this is what I charge, take it or leave it. If you value what I do you will pay me what I am worth. It sounds harsh but it has saved me from so much pain and wasted time. Other boundaries have included my private life and my time. I don't give away the time I want to spend with my family and don't feel the need to tell everyone everything about my personal life. These boundaries have given me the freedom to say no.

Say no

More often than not people pleasers struggle to say no. No is a very powerful word and it is acceptable to use it regularly. The ability to say no will set you free! Once you have accepted who you are and have set boundaries then no is a no-brainer. Some people will dislike you for saying no but on the whole you will find that most people will have more respect for you. In business, your ability to say no could be the best thing that happens to you as it could make you more in demand.

Learning these three little gems can save your life, it really can. People pleasing is the quickest way to fail at anything that you wish to succeed in. You have to stand out, not fit in.

"I don't know the recipe for success, but the key to failure is trying to please everybody."

People will speak against you

No matter how much you work at *not* being a people pleaser you will always have those who will speak against you. Whether you try hard to please them or try hard not to.

"Sometimes the person who tries to keep everyone else happy is the loneliest person."

The next degree of opposition is when people not only dislike you but will make sure that they tell everyone else about their dislike for you too. Hurt goes deeper at this stage and too many business owners become so discouraged that they give up. At this stage you need to become determined despite the opposition. Your skin needs to grow thicker whilst still keeping a soft heart towards all people. Even those who are speaking against you. If you can cultivate a heart of compassion towards people it will become a little easier. "See them as children," my husband always says to me. They are less mature and don't really understand what they are doing. What goes around comes around and if they are doing this to you then it will come back them. Just keep your own mouth clean and blameless so that what comes back to you is good. It is a skill to be learned but you can learn to deal with people who speak against you. Here are some things that I have learned along the way:

- Often it's all in our mind, people are not *always* saying bad things about you. Be careful of becoming too sensitive after one person has said something bad publicly.
- Before becoming upset talk to the person involved and where possible make peace with them. However, some people will not be reasonable so don't waste too much time on them if they aren't willing.
- Keep calm, don't react or you may say something you regret or something that can be used against you. Take time to think of a good response rather than a quick reaction.
- Kindness always wins. In any situation practice kindness despite how you may be feeling. Don't be discouraged though when your kindness is misinterpreted or used against you negatively. Unfortunately this does happen despite your best efforts.
- Ignore the insult, pretend like it never happened. Often the greatest insult is to not acknowledge the insult in the first place. Life is too short to respond to every attack or attacker.
- Pull in some reinforcement if things get out of hand. Ask your trusted followers to leave as much positive feedback as possible in the same

places that the negative feedback is being left. People are not stupid, they will see what is true and what is not. However, don't bring your positive followers down by sharing the negative with them, simply ask them for some feedback or a testimonial as you usually would in "normal" circumstances.

People will violently oppose you

This third degree of opposition is the most difficult one to deal with and few get past this stage. Proactive, violent opposition is not easy for anyone, even the thickest skinned person, to deal with. These battles often end up in court and can completely destroy a business or the business owner's sanity. It is ugly on every level and will leave scars no matter how nicely you try to deal with it. I am guessing that every single successful business owner that you look up to has such scars. Sadly, great business doesn't exist without getting past this stage. I can tell you some stories about this and how I came close to losing my company several times. Let me share one with you, it was long ago so shouldn't affect anyone involved.

She was on my team, I was very fond of her. I tend to get very attached to people, it's just how I am and I don't want to lose that part of my personality. I loved that she was extremely passionate about the Women's Business Club and was doing a brilliant job promoting it and getting ladies to come along to her club. Things were going well, she got our club in the newspaper, local celebrities came along to celebrate her/our success and business couldn't be any better.

Suddenly out of the blue she complained about having to attend a team meeting and that she wasn't willing to spend the time or money on it. Next she complained that I was micromanaging her when I asked her to stick to the franchise handbook. Before I knew what hit me she had reported me to the Franchise Association! I was gobsmacked. I loved her and invested my life in her. We celebrated her birthday together – she said no one else in her life had ever gone to as much trouble as I did to make her birthday special and she was touched. Regular thanks and gratitude came from her lips as she felt that she was lost before joining our team and then almost in the same breath she came against me with violent opposition. Naturally I was completely shocked! To this day I honestly don't know what happened, who poisoned her or what was going through her mind. It was a deep stab in my back which completely shook my confidence and desire to continue with the business. It ended up in a legal battle which I won, sadly. I say sadly because I won the battle but lost a friend. I would rather have lost the battle and kept a friend but even if I forfeited the battle, the friendship was clearly over from her side. This was quite some time ago and I have forgiven her, should she wish to come back and work with us again I would be more than willing to consider it on the condition that she would accept mentoring and give us time to rebuild trust.

I would like to tell you that this is the only such story I have to share but it isn't. There are more. I have many scars. Each person is still carried in my heart and I can still see their unrealised potential. Given half a chance I would take them back like a prodigal son and continue to invest in them until their full potential was flourishing. My husband says I have issues with letting go! I prefer to see it as never giving up on people no matter what. I genuinely love people. It's a quality that took me years to grow and one that I will not give up no matter how many scars it costs me. But where does that leave me today? Bitter, cold and unwilling to try again? Absolutely not. I forgive easily and move on quickly. These keys have helped me stay focused and not lose the business that I have worked so hard to build. I also admit that I was not without blame in any of the situations that gave me the scars. In every dispute there is always more than one person to blame. I accepted my part of the blame and used it to grow as a person.

"Great spirits have always encountered violent opposition from mediocre minds."

- Albert Einstein

Here are some things I learned from these violent oppositions:

- Salmon swim against the current. They swim upstream to fulfil their destiny! We too must recognise that there are few who have the strength and courage to go against the flow which is why so few succeed. It's easy to swim with the current like everyone else. I cannot be content with mediocrity so learned to swim upstream.

- Some people just like to fight. They have deeper issues or are deeply unhappy and will take it out on everyone else. I have learned to have compassion on such individuals whilst at the same time guarding my own heart, life and business.

- Times of opposition can be my best friend if I allow them to. They will always reveal my character flaws like nothing else will, so I can grow and improve. At times they will uncover insecurities and fears which I can deal with to find greater freedom. I have also learned that if I use opposition to understand people more I can have greater compassion and better people skills as a result.

The bottom line to all forms of opposition is that I can allow them to be either the making or the breaking of me. It's not the opposition that will choose but it's up to me. I have the power to choose to grow and learn or give up and quit. You have the same choice too!

I Did it Generously

"The world of the generous gets larger and larger; the world of the stingy gets smaller and smaller."

- Proverbs 11:24-25
The Message

The giver is happier than the getter.

I believe the wealthiest people on earth are not those who store up the most but those who allow the most to pass through their hands. This Christmas, yesterday actually, was the first Christmas in my life where I was in the financial position to give the gifts that I wanted to give to my friends and family. Each year I have struggled with a small budget to find a way to give good gifts for birthdays and Christmas. This year I had enough to get exactly what I wanted to get for each person and that freedom was amazing. Sleep eluded me on Christmas Eve as I was more excited than I had ever been at this time of year. My children were tucked up in bed fast asleep while I lay wide eyed and bushy tailed in excitement of what I was going to give in the morning! My excitement was centred around the fact that I *could* give and it was wonderful. Oh and what a joy it was to see everyone's faces as they got quality gifts, I loved every minute of it.

So why is the giver happier than the getter? The simplest explanation is to liken money to water. Water that is stored up gets stagnant and is no good to anyone but water that flows remains clean and offers a refreshing drink to many. I prefer to offer a drink to the thirsty than to create stagnant water which breeds germs and mosquitoes. Ultimately, I am also blessed by the fresh water while stagnant water only opens up a whole new set of problems that didn't exist before. If you wish to move away from the metaphor, consider that generosity is good for tax purposes – this is a great starting point for the argument of the benefits of being generous.

"We make a living by what we get. We make a life by what we give."

- Winston S. Churchill

Not too long ago I found myself sitting at a table with about twenty wealthy business owners. Bored with the traditional "So what do you do?" question, I decided to spice things up a little. Before the gentleman on my left had a chance to speak I quickly set up the tone for our conversation by very quickly saying, "Don't tell me what you do but rather, tell about what you do for fun." Once the initial shock of my unusual introduction passed, our conversation quickly turned to his love for an ancient game called Real Tennis. I had never heard of Real Tennis so he quickly went on to educate me about this form of tennis being the original racquet sport from which the modern game of lawn tennis or tennis is descended. The game has many complexities and the ball may bounce off a wall or sloped ceiling and is not simply played back and forth as it is in lawn tennis. The conversation was genuinely interesting and once we had shared our hobbies over a three course lunch we proceeded to tell each other what our business was. I recall that he was in the human resources industry. Instead of being another face in the sea of faces I meet every day, he stood out because I will always remember him for telling me about Real Tennis.

Then, turning to the gentleman seated at the head of the table, whose name was Tom (yes, the same Tom mentioned earlier), I asked the same question. His response was one that made me decide right then and there that I would no longer conduct business with him. In answer to my question about what he does for fun he replied, "I make money."

What You Sow, You Reap

So why did this response displease me to the extent that I did not want to do business with him? I firmly believe that anyone whose primary goal is to make money is trouble. People like this will stop at nothing to make their money and may even succeed in their quest for a while but in time they will fall and take many others down with them along the way. Making money is not a big enough *why*. Shortly after this lunch and my delightful education about Real Tennis, my theory was proven. Sadly, a friend of mine who had conducted business with Tom found herself in a legal battle with him which resulted in a significant financial loss for her. A few months later I met another lady who had a similar experience with Tom and had not only lost her entire life savings but she had also introduced Tom to her brother and he, too, lost everything. Tom's focus on money meant that he would stop at nothing to get what he wanted, even if it meant robbing everyone of every penny possible.   Tom is only one of many. I know of several business men and women who conduct business in a similar manner and absolutely ruin lives in the pursuit of wealth. Only time will tell but I can easily predict that at some point he will fall into his own trap and his money will not be sufficient to save him. What goes around comes around. What you sow, you reap.

Your *why* needs to be much bigger than the desire for a large bank balance. If you have a strong enough *why*, you will have what it takes to start with zero or minimal capital and you will have enough of a reason to get through the hard times.

Giving Makes You Happy

Harvard Business School professor Michael Norton conducted a study in 2008 and found that giving money to someone else lifted participants' happiness more that spending it on themselves (despite participants' prediction that spending on themselves would make them happier).

In a new book, *The Paradox of Generosity*, by sociologists Christian Smith and Hilary Davidson, research shows you'll be happier for giving. Americans who describe themselves as "very happy" volunteer an average of 5.8 hours per month. Those who are "unhappy"? Just 0.6 hours. This is just one of the findings in *The Paradox of Generosity*. Researchers for the initiative surveyed 2,000 individuals over a five-year period. They interviewed and tracked the spending habits and lifestyles of 40 families from different classes and races in 12 states.

"For it is in giving that we receive."

- Francis of Assisi

These happy feelings that result from generosity are reflected in our biology. In 2006 Jorge Moll and colleagues at the National Institute of Health conducted a study that discovered that when people give to charities, it activates regions of the brain associated with pleasure, social connection, and trust, creating a "warm glow" effect. Scientists also believe that selfless behaviour releases endorphins in the brain, producing the happy feeling known as the "helper's high".

I believe that one of the reasons that we see so much business growth and joy in the Women's Business Clubs across the UK is because we encourage the ladies to help and support each other –to give to each other.

The results speak for themselves! It is good business sense to be generous not only with giving financially to charities but also with time so support people when they need you. Balance of course is key or else you can spend all your time helping others and never do what is required in your business.

7 Ways to Help Yourself by Helping Others

1. Referrals

It doesn't take much make to make an introduction. A simple email introduction or bluetoothing a contact across takes a mere second or two. However, the impact that these few seconds make is huge and as I keep saying, what you sow you will reap. Become known for someone who makes referrals and this will always put you at the top of the list to receive referrals. So do whatever you can to always be connecting people with each other.

2. Sponsorship

Find events, charities or small businesses who need support and offer to be a sponsor in return for having your brand attached to any marketing they do in that area. A small investment will really help them get to the next level of success and not only will you be known as generous but your brand will also get out further afield.

3. Gifts

At the Women's Business Club we find any and every excuse to give gifts! Gifts make the recipient feel good and they are so much fun for the giver. The gift doesn't necessarily have to be extravagant to have an impact. We give gifts for each and every referral as a thank you, we celebrate birthdays and just about anything else we can think of. Making someone feel good will make you memorable over your competitors. People don't always remember what you say but they always remember how you made them feel. Give gifts to make yourself and others feel good.

4. Time

It is very common these days to hear, "I don't have enough time!" More often than not I hear people using lack of time as a complaint or an excuse. I have only ever met one person in business who didn't make me feel bad for taking up her time; she gave me the impression that she had all the time in the world for me both before, during and after selling me my Lexus. She inspired me to stop being so rushed and to start being more peaceful. She even had the same manner about her during March, the busiest month of the year for car sales.

Do you give away some of your time to help people or are you too busy? Giving money away is probably easier than giving time away so when you do give your time away people really notice. Take time out of your busy schedule to be kind to someone, to really listen to people and to help people who need your time. Once again, what you sow you will reap and your time will come back to you in the most unexpected ways.

5. Resources

Do you share what you have or do you hold on tightly to it? Do you feel that by sharing you will lose and give your competitors the advantage? It's quite the contrary, the business owners who do not feel insecure and threatened, who share freely without fear, are the ones who gain the most respect and admiration.

6. Listening

How many people really listen these days? Have you noticed how superficial our conversations have become? Do you know that most people like to talk about themselves and will be so grateful to the person who actually allows them to? In most networking events I cringe as each person I speak to waffles through their sales pitch and attempts to tell me all about their business and how much I need them. What they don't do is first ask me about myself to discover if I actually even need anything that they have to offer. The person in the room who takes time to listen is the one who will end up with the most business!

7. Donations

Yes I said it. Give away your money! Not only is it good for tax purposes but it is good for your soul to do something meaningful in this world. You don't only have to donate hard cash, you can also donate resources. For example, I know of a charity here in Cheltenham that sends computers to schools in Africa: when you upgrade your computer why not donate the old one to a charity such as this. There is so much good that can be done in this world with just a little bit of giving from everyone.

Generosity will always be rewarded one way or another, so don't be too afraid or too stingy to give it a go. If your competitors are generous and you are not then guess who has the upper hand and will go further faster?

The Success Secret

The Women's Business Club is probably the fastest growing women's business network in the UK. We have grown from zero to 12 thriving clubs in just over one year with many more launches in the pipeline. Women grow and thrive in our clubs and more often than not we see miraculous growth not only in their business but also in their confidence. The secret to our success is one very simple thing, relationships. To build effective and genuine relationships you have to give up some time. We do not encourage hard selling but we do encourage the women to take time to get to know each other. The results have been phenomenal!

We have seen and proven that relationships build sustainable businesses.

So why are relationships so powerful? I believe and have seen evidence to my beliefs that relationships offer the following benefits that good old fashioned hard selling or cold calling lacks:

Loyalty

If you are using any of the hard sales methods you might win a sale but you are unlikely to win the person. As soon as you lean in for the kill people tend to back off. It might have worked in times past but people are so accustomed to this method now that it is mostly off-putting. Taking time to develop a relationship means that you win the person and once you have won the person you have won a lifetime of sales.

People buy from people. If they like you they are more likely to buy from you. It's not rocket science, it's just human nature. At Women's Business Club we have worked very hard at crafting our culture around this one secret. We have seen over and over again that the women who come to our clubs simply to sell seldom make sales, give up and don't return. But those who come and connect with the other women and get to know them are thriving because of the loyalty and support of the other members. I am certain that our Women's Business Club ladies will do most of their Christmas shopping from other club members this year because they get so much more delight from supporting each other's businesses than they would ever get from buying from a large chain. Also, I am encouraging them to do so! You could not get these kinds of sales from hard selling or cold calling, and this is the result of the loyalty that is formed through relationships.

We live in such a fast paced, instant messaging, short sentenced (140 characters or less), online, microwave society that too many have stopped taking the time to cultivate quality relationships – especially in business. Are we taking time to understand people? Are we matching needs to solutions or are we trying to shove our businesses down other people's throats whether they need it or not? In my passion and enthusiasm for what I do I have been guilty of doing just that. I have assumed that every business woman I meet needs every single service I offer. After making quite a few mistakes I quickly realised that not everyone needs me and my insistence that they did was very off putting for them. I cringe when I think of some of the things I have said and done to make a sale when I first started!

– I have been guilty of over promising just to make a sale and then not being able to deliver. I have since learnt to under promise and over deliver so that my clients are super impressed that I exceeded their expectations.

– I have been guilty of undercharging or doing favours and freebies just to make a sale. I have since learned that people value what they have to pay for and I was selling myself short in my desperation to sell. Now our prices are set because we are worth every penny.

– I have been guilty of focusing on the sale and not the person which meant I didn't treat people in the way I should have. I have since learned that if you treat people right and value them then the sales will come at the right time and in the right way. And they will keep coming over and over again because people do need to feel respected.

Collaboration

Relationships in business either B2B or B2C can lead to exciting ideas, partnerships, collaboration and synergy. Two are better than one. There is no business owner that is skilled in every area of business. We all have strengths and weaknesses. We all have fears and insecurities. We are all part of a great big business jigsaw puzzle. It's obvious that if you are willing to find your fit and be a part of the big picture that you will do very well. At the Women's Business Club we have seen some amazing results in this area. Several women have partnered together because they realised that their success was limited on their own and that their chances were far great if they worked with other women. Businesses are growing and thriving as a result of these sorts of relationships.

Referrals

Referrals are when other people use their time and effort to help you build your business. Why would someone bother to do that? If someone tried a particular brand of shampoo for example they might point you to anyone who sells that shampoo instead of directly to your business which offers the same product. However, when the relationship becomes personal the recommendation becomes personal. Now that person will point directly to you. Relationships encourage referrals. Word of mouth is so powerful, especially in our social media age. If used wisely, social media can grow any business as people talk about what they love and hate on social media.

Generosity builds relationships. A generous person is attractive and irresistible. Who would not want to be in the company of someone who is generous? In fact, correct me if I am wrong, but I believe that generosity and kindness go hand in hand. You cannot be generous without being kind hearted and who would not want to be with a kind and generous person? Based on this assumption then, generosity is a no brainer to building a business.

If you are generous and your competitors are not, where do you think the customers would prefer to go? My life is rich with generous people and I do my best to be as generous as possible too. An emotional connection results after doing business with generous people and this emotional connection is what will keep your customers loyal.

To end off, I would like to mention that generosity needs to be sincere and come from the heart because you care about what or who you are giving to. If you give to get back you are not being generous but merely strategic and that sort of giving will not offer the same results that sincere, kind generosity will. If you struggle with generosity that's OK, being aware of this is much better than being blind to it. Grow your generosity "muscle" by practicing. Give some money to a charity or time to a person without expecting anything back. At first it may hurt a little but in time you will love the euphoria that results from being generous and before you realise it, you will see your relationships and business grow. You may even find people start giving generously to you.

About The Author

ANGELA DE SOUZA is the director of a fast growing national franchise, the Women's Business Club. She is a passionate entrepreneur, wife, mother of four beautiful children, speaker, author, and song writer just for fun. Angela has a passion to see women reach their full potential and offers a great deal of support to many through Women's Business Club.

About the Women's Business Club

At the Women's Business Club we support women in their businesses and our top priority is building relationships. We support women through one on one mentoring, through network events and through our business growth workshops. We simply offer great business training and facilitate relationships. That's it. We hope that the experiences shared in this book has inspired you in some way and if there is anything that we can do to support you in your business please get in touch with one of our team at www.womensbusiness.club

Other Books *by* Angela

Emotional Gravity

What Goes Up Must Come Down

Do you feel a constant pull in your life but cannot explain what it is? It is gravity on your physical body but there is also emotional gravity pulling on your soul! Life is constantly in motion. Life never stands still and will always involve change. The sooner you accept this reality, the sooner you will be able to lead a life without too many disappointments.

Being You

The most powerful thing that you have to offer the world is the authentic you. You are indisputably original. Understanding your value will unlock your potential and take you to places that you never dreamed possible. Are you tired of the same old, same old? Are you yearning for more out of life? Feel you can do so much better than you are? The great news is that the answer is not to be found in a pot of gold at the end of a rainbow. The answer is inside of YOU! Being You shows you exactly how you can begin your journey of self discovery and capitalise on your very own exclusive, unique brand – the authentic you! Get ready to turn your life around completely and live life the way you were meant to, simply by being you!

Christian and Arabella

A Love Stronger Than Anything Imaginable

A chance meeting between Christian and Arabella results in a truly captivating tale of unlikely, but eternal, undying love. Upper class Christian can have any woman he chooses, and yet, his heart belongs to Arabella, a "common" girl who couldn't be more undeserving of the affection, undying commitment and yearning love that Christian showers on her. Arabella is oblivious to Christian's unconditional love for her and instead chooses a life of debauchery. Her life quickly spirals completely out of control until she reaches the lowest point one can possibly reach. Death stared her in the face many times and yet, a guardian angel watched over her every step of the way. Facing rejection, betrayal and completely hopeless circumstances, Christian chooses to fight in the name of love, with nothing more than a glimmer of hope to keep him going. This is a tale of one man's determination to capture the heart of the woman he loves in the face of impossibility; to overcome every obstacle in his way and give his life up, if he has to, for the woman who holds the key to his heart. This is the tale of a woman, who through making one wrong decision early in life, chose the path leading to self-destruction and utter despair, paying a high price along the way. This is a tale of an unlikely romance that held on from burnt, dying ashes, to a spark, and eventually a flame of unshakeable, unquenchable love, a love that would conquer anything.

Maximise

Women's BUSINESS **CONFERENCE** & AWARDS

Inspiring, Empowering & Equipping UK Business Women

BOOK NOW £12.50
www.maximiseconference.co.uk

Business Stands | Workshops | Speakers | Dragon's Den | Awards | Networking